THE ESCAPING HABIT

The Escaping Habit

by

JOSEPH ORNA

with

HUGH POPHAM

LEO COOPER
IN ASSOCIATION WITH
SECKER & WARBURG

I dedicate this book to Brother Domenico Falcone, to whom I owe my freedom, given to me at the risk of his life, and to the many good people who helped me on my way.

First published in Great Britain 1975 by
LEO COOPER LTD
Republished 1986 by Leo Cooper
in association with Secker & Warburg Ltd
54 Poland Street, London W1V 3DF

ISBN 0 436 34120 4

Printed in Great Britain by
St Edmundsbury Press, Bury St Edmunds, Suffolk

Prologue

WHEN anyone asks me how I, a cockney from Clerkenwell, was able to travel for a whole year through wartime Italy disguised as a monk and never get caught, my answer is, 'A lot of luck, certainly, but also my upbringing, and the varied life I'd led.' My family came originally from Switzerland, but settled in London before the First World War. My father was a tailor; but although the going was rough, we were a singularly happy and united family, and my mother saw to it that we never went hungry or barefoot, as did many of the children in our street in those years before the war. We were Catholics; and I used to attend the local church, and took part in the services as an altar-boy. This experience, which I never completely forgot, came in very useful; and in Italy I was to have living proof that Catholicism is still a truly international faith, transcending differences of race and language.

When I was 14 I left school and, being encouraged to follow my father's trade, began my apprenticeship to a tailor in the West End. This was 1922 and wages were very low: my father, as a master-craftsman, only earned about thirty-five shillings a week: and when a pal suggested that I should do better as a waiter, I decided to have a try.

My first job was in Soho. That colourful square mile of London was as cosmopolitan then as it is today; and in the restaurants and kitchens where I worked, I mixed with French, Italians, Greeks, Germans and many other nationalities,

5

and quickly picked up a smattering of their languages. I also learnt that a good waiter is an actor who conceals his feelings towards the customers he serves, however keenly he detests them, and always presents the same air of detached, yet personal, concern for their comfort and well-being. Equally he must keep a cool head – not always easy, either, when he is being rushed off his feet, and, at the same time, is being called or beckoned by half a dozen people at once.

For all that, I liked the work, and relished the atmosphere of wealth and sophistication, as I saw it from my humble position; the men in their well-cut evening clothes, the beautiful women in their expensive gowns and furs and jewels. It was another world from the mean streets I returned to in the early hours of the morning. I didn't feel particularly envious; but I very much wanted to acquire a share of the world's good things for myself. I suppose, like many young men from my sort of background, I wanted to 'better myself'. At the same time, I had a longing for adventure, to see a bit more of the world. And so, in 1926, I left London and signed on as a steward with the Blue Star Line.

For the next few years I worked aboard many of the famous trans-Atlantic liners, the old *Aquitania* and *Mauretania*, and also the ships of the Canadian Pacific. To some extent these voyages assuaged my yearning for travel and adventure, but I was always ready for something new; and when I heard that waiters were wanted for the Royal York Hotel in Toronto, which was just about to open, I volunteered and was accepted.

As it turned out, the job was by no means as good as had been made out, and I only stayed six weeks; I moved on to Niagara Falls where I made the acquaintance of an American hotelier, Mr Borbey, who offered me a post in New York – if I could get there.

At that time immigration into the States was strictly controlled under the quota system, and there was little chance of my getting a work permit. But there were other ways of entering the country. With almost my last few bucks, I went to the Falls View Bridge that links Canada and the States, and, arranging with a sympathetic American to carry my bags, strolled across.

'Where ya going, bud?' asked the official on the American side.

'Just for a meal, and maybe a movie,' I said. 'I'll be back this evening.'

'Okay,' he said, and waved me through.

As soon as I was out of his sight I collected my grips and headed for New York. When I'd bought my ticket, I had exactly twenty-five cents left. I was to pay a stiff price for that light-hearted bit of law-breaking later on. But Mr Borbey was as good as his word, and gave me a job in the Lexington Hotel. Here, and elsewhere in New York, I began to get the feel of earning good money.

These were the years of prohibition, when bootleg liquor was big business, and the gangsters who ran the rackets and owned and operated the speakeasies where it was sold, thrived and grew rich. Many of these joints were not the sleazy dens of popular imagination, but luxurious clubs patronized by the famous and the wealthy, by anyone, in fact, who needed a drink and could afford to pay for it. But this did not prevent them being regularly raided by the police.

Through my American contacts, I was given an introduction into this underworld, and soon found myself waiting in one of the most famous, the Central Park Casino. The money was good, the tips were lavish, and the fact that my employers were gangsters didn't bother me at all. Here, and later on in Chicago, I was on nodding terms with many of the most notorious gunmen of the time, Al Capone, 'Legs' Diamond, etc. I worked under the name of Joe Travers.

When a joint was raided, the staff were normally able to

make their escape via the back door; but if you were caught and convicted, the boss had to pay a fifty-dollar fine, and with a police record the chances of getting another job in the speakeasies were slight. The bosses simply didn't want to know. For several years I was lucky and was able to stash away a tidy sum in the bank. My ambitions of wealth and the good life were beginning to seem a little less fantastic; I was 21; I was gaining wide and varied experience in my chosen profession; I had good clothes and money in my pocket. I daresay I was a bit cocky; but who isn't at that age? I had visions of one day having a club of my own, in New York or London, and mixing on equal terms with my wealthy patrons. So much for dreams.

*

The night they raided Central Park Casino I made my getaway up the servery lift and out through a window, and so back to my room. The raid had finally decided me to leave New York: now, on the spur of the moment, I made up my mind to go that very night. I would take a train from Grand Central Station and head west in search of 'fresh woods and pastures new'. I packed my bags, and then, in one of those trivial decisions which alter one's whole life, I went along the corridor to take a bath before I set off.

I was in the tub when I heard a heavy banging on the front door and the unmistakable harsh voice of the New York cops.

'Police! Open up!'

I waited, listening intently behind the locked door. After a time they came tramping up to my floor. I heard the name Travers: and then they passed the bathroom on the way to my room. How had they got on to me? Then I remembered the waiters' roster by the chef's office: it had all our names and addresses on it.

Desperately, I tried to work out a plan of action. I had only my dressing-gown and a towel – no outfit in which to take to the streets! – and it was only a matter of minutes before they tried the bathroom. My only hope was to hide somewhere while they searched my room, then, when they'd gone, slip back and pick up my bags. But where?

Silently I let myself out of the bathroom and tip-toed along the corridor, away from my own room. I knew a girl on the same floor: a cute redhead by the name of Kitty Shannon, who was the room-service telephonist at the Lexington. She would let me take refuge with her until the cops had gone.

'Kitty! Kitty! I'm in bad trouble! Kitty!' I knocked softly on her door, and after a few seconds that seemed like several hours, she opened up and let me in.

In a few words I told her the problem. Without hesitation, she opened the clothes closet, shoved me inside and closed the door. I was still there, among all the dresses and petticoats and furs, when the cops, who had decided to search the house for me and tried the bathroom in vain, burst in, wrenched open the closet door and hauled me out.

Kitty displayed convincing amazement, and I swore blind that I had hidden there while she was out of the room. The cops were indifferent; they had their man; and I was frog-marched off to the police station to be given a taste of New York rough justice. They cross-questioned me savagely, disclosing that they knew that my name was not Travers and that I had no work permit, roughed me up, and slung me into the notorious Tombs gaol, where I shared a cell with every species of drunk, drug-addict and hoodlum, and where, when I asked one of the guards to change five dollars so that I could make a phone call, he gave me a dime and pocketed the note.

'Why, kid, you ain't going no place,' he said, when I protested.

9

The ensuing three months were some of the most depressing of my life, though they do not take long to recount. The lawyer they recommended me was crooked, and charged me a retaining fee of 500 dollars; my bail cost me another thousand; and when I came out of gaol, I couldn't get work. The system knew what had happened and black-listed me; others thought I was a stool pigeon and refused to employ me; at one joint I was sacked after my lawyer phoned me there: 'We don't want nothin' to do wid lawyers,' I was told.

To make matters worse – and reduce my own troubles to insignificance – Wall Street had crashed, and the streets of New York were thronged with queues of unemployed, shuffling on the daily breadline. I had no option but to join them. On my lawyer's advice, I was persuaded to defend my case: I should have done much better to let them deport me via the lazaretto of Ellis Island. Then the lawyer could not have skinned me alive, as he proceeded to do. I was his meal ticket.

Week after week the case dragged on. Each time it came up, it was, once more, adjourned; and each time the lawyer claimed another slice of my precious savings, for he had my bank book. To cut a long story short, at the end of three months I appeared once more in court. This time there was a different judge; and I was so desperate that, when the defence was called, I stood up, ignoring the frantic signals of my lawyer, and blurted out the story of my misfortunes. The judge listened sympathetically, and when I had finished, he dismissed the case, adding some pointed comments upon the way in which it had been handled.

*

I was a free man at last, but unemployable, and broke, for I was unable to recover my 1,000 dollars bail, and the lawyer extracted all the rest of the little money I had left. There was nothing for it but to stow away on the first ship I could find bound for England.

Down at the docks, the only White Star alongside was the *Olympic*, and I had never sailed in her. However, by chance I ran into a man I knew, the linen-keeper, Marcel, from a previous ship. He agreed to help me. While he arranged to get my bags aboard, I strolled over the gangway like any other member of the crew, and found Marcel, who put me in the linen-room. But not for long.

The heat! It might be all right for sheets and bedspreads, but it was obvious that I shouldn't survive in that temperature for the next six hours, let alone the next six days; so I let myself out and went exploring. I discovered that the kosher cook was also an old shipmate of mine; unfortunately he was already harbouring one stowaway and had his hands full; so I decided to fend for myself.

The ship was fairly empty that trip, and scouting around, I soon found an unlocked, empty cabin – No 48, 'C' Deck; I've never forgotten it! – and simply occupied it. I knew the drill sufficiently well to satisfy the cabin steward, if he should ask any questions; but I still had the problem of eating.

It was then I had a stroke of luck. Up on deck I happened to get into conversation with one of the 2nd Class passengers, a first-generation Albanian immigrant of my own age on his way home to visit his relatives, and as lonely as I was. We had a drink together, and he suggested that as we were both on our own, and he had a spare berth in his cabin, I should move in with him. Nothing could have suited me better. He arranged it with his steward; and immediately I became simply another passenger, eating in the saloon with him, strolling the decks, drinking my mid-morning beef-tea. On one occasion, with four Greek acquaintances, we made a foray into the forbidden territory of the 1st Class.

The Master-at-Arms saw us, and sent the other four packing.

'Look like a bunch of stowaways,' he said confidentially to us, when they had gone sheepishly back to 2nd Class. 'You two are all right; have a good look round!'

In this manner I had a very pleasant voyage home, by courtesy of White Star – though they weren't aware of it. When we docked at Southampton, I 'borrowed' a steward's uniform and, carrying my bags as if they belonged to one of the passengers, was the second man ashore. I changed in the lavatory, touched Laurie, the French restaurant waiter, for a pound, and bought a ticket to London, where my mother was immensely surprised to see me.

'Lend me a quid,' I said, as soon as we had embraced.

'You're back all right!' she said, going for her purse.

After four years away, determined to make my fortune, I was back in England with even less money than when I had set off, but the richer for a whole range of experiences, some of which I could well have done without. I immediately set about looking for work, and soon landed a job at Kate Merrick's famous night club, The Bobbin, in Regent Street, where, as in the speakeasies in New York, the tipping was liberal, and police raids were by no means uncommon – though they were bribed to warn us when they were coming. In fact, there were three while I was there: at the first warning, the waiters scooped up bills and cash from the tables and scarpered.

It was a good billet, all the same, and did something to restore my shattered finances. But after a time my feet started to itch once more, and I went back to sea, first in the Union Castle Line, running to South Africa, then in boats running to South America. After a year or two I had managed to save quite a bit, and with a pal I decided to open a club in London.

This was in 1938, not the best year to choose for launching a new enterprise; and when the war started, we abandoned

it, and I went back to my old trade, taking a job at the
Quo Vadis, in Frith Street.

*

That autumn saw the start of the blitz. It did not suit
my temperament to sit and 'take it', as Londoners were
credited with doing, and after a second winter of bombing
I decided I had to get away from it at all costs. So one day
in January 1942 I went down to the Ministry of War
Transport offices by the Pool of London and said I was
looking for a ship.

The clerk shrugged. 'Nothing doing here, mate. Try
upstairs.'

I duly went upstairs and repeated my request, this time
to an officer.

'Want a ship, do you?' he said, glancing at my ticket
of discharge. 'Right. Sign here.'

Without giving the matter any thought, I signed the form
he pushed in front of me.

'Right, my lad. You've got a ship. You're in the navy.'

I was flabbergasted. 'In the navy?'

'That's right. You're a T124X rating, attached to the
RN. You'll draw Merchant Service rates of pay, and you'll
be posted as Steward/Gunner to either a naval or a merchant
ship. Any questions?'

I couldn't think of any offhand, I was too surprised;
and a few weeks later I was instructed to join the mine-
sweeper *Agamemnon*, then at Gourock. Within a matter of
days we joined a convoy heading for Gibraltar, and from
there went on into the Mediterranean. And that is where
my story really begins.

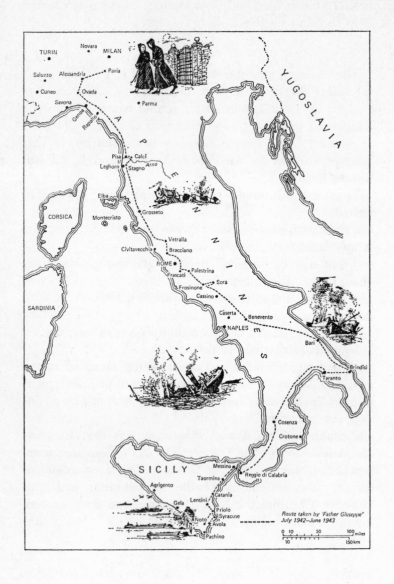

TURIN

Novara MILAN

Saluzzo Alessandria Pavia

Cuneo Ovada

Savona

Genoa

Rapallo

Parma

YUGOSLAVIA

Pisa Calci
Leghorn Stagno
Arno

Elba

CORSICA Montecristo

Grosseto

Vetralla

Civitavecchia Bracciano

ROME Palestrina
Frascati
Frosinone Sora
Cassino

SARDINIA

Càserta Benevento

NAPLES

Bari

Brindisi

Taranto

Cosenza
Crotone

SICILY

Messina
Taormina Reggio di Calabria

Agrigento Catania
Gela Lentini
Priolo
Noto Syracuse
Avola
Pachino

Route taken by 'Father Giuseppe'
July 1942–June 1943

0 10   50   100 miles
10   150km

Chapter One

JUNE of 1942 in the Mediterranean was glorious, and life aboard so far had been remarkably peaceful, considering the area we were working. Our job was to keep the sea lanes between Sicily and North Africa clear of mines for the convoys which were being fought through from Gibraltar to Malta and Alexandria, and to besieged Tobruk.

I was on watch, manning an oerlikon cannon. My mind should have been on my job, but at sea, in war or peace, one's thoughts tend to wander towards the pleasures of life ashore. A nice spell of leave in Alexandria or the Fleet Club in Cairo, or a day on the beach at Sidi Bisch – that was the direction my daydreams took. It was at Sidi Bisch that I had met Madalene. What a girl. She'd taken every last penny I had, as I had known she would, but I hadn't cared . . . I was a sailor on leave.

I was brought sharply back to the present by the sound of 'Action Stations'. We were sweeping ahead of a twenty-ship convoy bound for Tobruk, and we had been expecting attack by both aircraft and U-boats. Here it came. The escorts were circling the convoy blazing away with their ack-ack. There were enemy aircraft all round us. Some of the ships had already been hit, and their crews were abandoning them. We started to pick up survivors, a heart-breaking job; men badly burned, delirious with pain; men spewing up oil; one, with a shattered arm, in convulsions from the oil he had swallowed. I put my finger down his throat to help him heave it up. I thought he was dying, but the spasms passed and he lay still, exhausted but relieved.

The fighting continued without respite; the enemy must have put every aircraft he possessed into the air for this one. The convoy had suffered severely. Our sick bay was busy, for we had doubled our complement with the survivors. We were all exhausted. The guns were too hot to touch. I knew for sure that I had got one aircraft. It was a Stuka, and as it was climbing away after its attack, I followed it, firing all the time. I could see my tracers stitching into it; then it blew up, showering pieces down around us.

An Italian torpedo bomber, coming in low, misjudged the swell, hit a wave with his wing-tip, and crashed. I was watching a destroyer manœuvring to pick up the crew, when a tremendous explosion hurled me from my seat at the oerlikon, knocking me senseless. When I came to, it was to find complete devastation. We had taken one hit amidships, and another in our aft magazine, and the whole ship was on fire. Some of our guns were still in action, but the injured were already being loaded into boats and rafts and cast off from the side. Enemy planes were strafing the crippled ship and the water round us. Lifeboats and rafts were being sunk as soon as they pulled away.

The order came to abandon ship. The fires were out of control, and those who were still able to, helped the helpless into the boats. I made my way forward and found some of my mates; together we went over the side and towards one of the rafts. There wasn't room for all of us, so we took turns, those in the water helping to guide the raft by swimming behind and pushing it shorewards. Luckily for us, we were no more than half-a-mile or so from the beach, but it was quite far enough.

*

We reached the shore after about an hour, more dead

than alive, and joined up with other survivors. There was nothing for us to do but muck in with the British troops defending Tobruk; but it was hardly an attractive prospect. Supplies and ammunition were running low, and small arms were in short supply; but we helped as best we could. How long we would last was anybody's guess.

My contact with the enemy up to this time had consisted of listening to an occasional broadcast by Lord Haw-Haw, and, once in a while, sighting reconnaissance aircraft. Now, here I was, facing the Afrika Korps on dry land, and I found I had no desire to meet them, socially or otherwise. I was also learning what a tough job the army had; there was no relief from the shelling; and Tobruk itself was a shambles, with fires everywhere, streets choked with rubble, the harbour strewn with wrecked ships. And there was no way out; it was simply a trap.

There was a brief respite in the bombardment, then the big German guns started up again with intensified fury. Shells were exploding all round us, the air above was buzzing with shrapnel; aircraft strafed us. I was wounded in the arm; someone, I never knew who, put on a tourniquet to staunch the bleeding. Lennie, the farm boy, was lying next to me. He was hurt too. He was six foot four and broad to match, yet as gentle as a lamb and very naïve. He was only 19 and had been brought up in an orphanage, and from there he had gone to a farm. He had a disproportionate respect for those of us who had 'been around'; Nugget, who was only five feet five, and was so called because of his one gold tooth, right in the front; Ace, the first-class card player; Harry the Horse, another farm boy; Scouse, the Liverpudlian; myself, known as The Saint. As shipmates, we had had some great times together in Alexandria, Cairo, Suez, Malta and back in England. Now we were in the thick of it and we intended to stick together.

The army were outnumbered and outgunned, and there

17

was no chance of a relief column, as there would be in the films. After four days the inevitable end came. Tobruk fell, and we were taken prisoner.

*

After two days behind the wire, we were herded on board a transport. We arrived in Naples during the first week of June. The relief of getting off the ship was short-lived, as we were marched straight to the station and bundled into a cattle train, forty to a truck. Our destination, we were told, was Campo 303 near Pavia, a town about 25 miles south of Milan in the north of Italy. Compared to the train, the ship had been a luxury liner.

Pavia is 400 miles from Naples and the journey took us the best part of three days. We stopped once a day to eat and stretch our legs, but we were never out of the train for more than fifteen minutes at a time. The stench was overpowering. If it had been winter it wouldn't have been so bad, but the heat of the Italian sun intensified the smell a hundred times.

When we arrived we were greeted by Germans. Up to now our guards had been mainly Italian; the only Germans we had seen had been the crew of the ship, and the attendants in the field kitchens they had set up in the stations on the way to Pavia. From the station we were marched to Campo 303. The streets were lined with curious civilians who jeered and taunted us, and when Scouse made some comment to a girl, a German soldier gave him a shove with his rifle that sent him staggering. That made me realize we were prisoners. Up to now we hadn't been maltreated, except for overcrowding and bad food; but this little bit of violence brought the cold facts home to me.

We reached the camp without further incidents and were marched to various huts which were dotted around the compound. This was some place. A double barbed wire fence, with a six-foot gap between, and twenty feet high, surrounded the entire area. Every fifty yards there was a tower with a machine-gun, which was manned continuously, and a powerful searchlight. I could hear dogs barking, and two German soldiers passed, each leading a Dobermann Pinscher. The dogs were straining at their leashes and barking and growling at us; they had obviously been trained to tear PoWs apart. I'd never really been afraid of dogs, but I was scared stiff of those two brutes.

At each hut forty of us were pulled out of the formation and motioned inside. They were bare except for a double row of bunks along the walls, and one pot-bellied stove at each end. We paired off and chose our bunks. Nugget and I stayed together and he, being shorter, took the bottom one. Two guards remained in the hut with us. They were both Italian, which was some relief. They didn't say anything, but took the opportunity for a smoke break. As soon as we were settled, we were paraded and marched to the wash hut. There were double rows of sinks, toilets and, to our amazement, showers. We stripped off and got straight in. After the filth of the journey the water felt marvellous; and even though the soap was caustic and burned our skin, we didn't care. To be clean and fresh again was worth a little discomfort.

One of the guards assigned to our hut became friendly with us. His name was Carlo, and he spoke some English. Through him we managed to get the lighter duties of the camp, and he made sure that we were first in the mess hall and the wash house. To anyone who hasn't been in captivity this may not seem much, but to us they were most important benefits.

From the moment of being caught, I started to think about escaping. I talked about it constantly to Nugget and the others whom I knew I could trust, but they thought it was crazy, and that I should never make it. Their scepticism only hardened my determination. I felt that, as a last resort, I might conceivably get help from some of the Italian guards; but, in fact, salvation came in a different guise altogether.

Chapter Two

THERE was a monk, Brother Domenico, who used to come regularly to the camp to give Mass, and to comfort those who needed it. As a Catholic, I naturally went to Mass, and struck up a friendship with him. We used to walk round the compound together; and on one of these occasions he suggested we organized a sports programme. He got us a football, and the inter-hut games we played were a great morale booster.

Sometimes, young girls would come to the fence and taunt us. This was not at all good for morale, however much Fra Domenico might preach about the sin of evil thoughts. We were normal, healthy young men, and our thoughts, if evil, were entirely natural.

From time to time, another monk by the name of Fra Filipo, accompanied Fra Domenico; and I noticed that they both came and went as they pleased. They simply walked up to the gates, the guards would open up, and after making the sign of the Cross, the two monks would walk through unchallenged. Through the guard, Carlo, I started to learn Italian, and I was able to practise with Fra Domenico and some of the other guards. It was a northern dialect, which was a higher form of the language than that spoken in the south.

I was lying in bed one night, brooding, as usual, on the problem of escaping, when, with a flash of inspiration, the way out came to me. I was so excited, I woke Nugget and told him my plan.

'Oh, forget it. Go back to sleep!' he said. 'It's crazy.'

The others, when I told them next day, were equally discouraging.

'It won't work,' they said, 'and if they catch you, you'll be shot.'

I pleaded with Nugget to come with me, but he wouldn't, so I told him I'd do it alone. My plan was simplicity itself. I would dress as a monk and walk out of the compound, just as Fra Domenico and Fra Filipo did. I realized I would need Fra Domenico's co-operation, but I didn't think he'd refuse. In this I was a little too optimistic. When I told him of my idea the following day and asked for his help, he wouldn't hear of it. Not on patriotic or moral grounds, but because he was afraid he would be jeopardizing my life. I couldn't convince him that the idea, and consequently the responsibility, would be entirely mine. It was a severe blow, and for several days I felt utterly despondent. I avoided my friends – and I avoided Fra Domenico.

Self-pity is a sterile emotion, and at last I pulled myself together. The next time I saw Fra Domenico I went to him and asked him to forgive me. Among other things, I was worried that he might have told the camp commandant; but he assured me that he would never do such a thing. He didn't offer to help, but restricted himself to telling me to pray. He showed no resentment at my request, and I felt better. I went and apologized to Nugget and Ace and the few others I had told; and although nothing had changed, suddenly I felt on top of the world.

For a time life settled back into the dull routine of prison camp. The games of football became boring, and the girls, still hanging around the wire, made our lives even more wretched. We had names for most of them—'Fat Falocci', 'The Shrimp', 'Nottingham May' – and some of them were real cows – a case of the cows outside, and the bulls inside!

In spite of my setback, my thoughts were still on escape.

There was a lot of talk, the usual things, tunnels and so forth; but, to me, my idea seemed the most feasible, if only I could get it set up. The camp was very crowded now, as other units had been sent there from North Africa, where the Afrika Korps were taking heavy toll of the Allies. We found that we had been reported 'Missing in Action', which would give no comfort to our families.

I resumed my walks with Fra Domenico. He didn't refer to my suggestion, but he did tell me how the war was progressing. Then, one day, he asked if we could go to the hut. I anticipated another pep-talk, but instead, we sat and talked of general things until some other prisoners who were present had left. As soon as we were alone, he produced from the folds of his habit a crucifix and a pair of sandals of the same type as he was wearing himself. I didn't grasp the significance of the sandals; but the crucifix gave me some comfort and I never let it out of my sight.

*

The 27th of July, 1942, was a Sunday: it is a date I shall not easily forget. I had been at Campo 303 for six weeks. The two monks came as usual to the camp to say Mass, and afterwards Fra Domenico and I fell into our usual custom of conversation. Without my realizing it, he was edging me towards my hut; when we reached the door, he suggested we went inside out of the sun. Aussie, Len, Ace and Nugget were all there, cleaning their belongings and sprucing the place up. Being Sunday, it was a free day and we could do pretty well what we liked.

We sat on my bunk and Fra Domenico asked if I had given any further thoughts to escaping.

'I think about little else,' I said. 'It's the only thing that keeps me going. Why?'

I had become so convinced that he wouldn't help me that I took it to be a routine question. He went on:

23

'If you were to get out of the camp, where would you make for?'

This gave me a jolt, for I realized then that I had no plans, other than for getting through the gate. I didn't know where Pavia was on the map except that it was three days by train from Naples. And I didn't know if Naples was north, south, east or west of Pavia. I hedged, saying that I was prepared to rely on my determination, plus my smattering of Italian. Fra Domenico was non-committal, and when he said, 'Well, I must get along. I've others to see,' I realized I'd been right. He'd just been showing polite interest in my problems.

Then, without a word, without warning, he reached inside his habit and pulled out one identical to it, and quickly stuffed it underneath my mattress before anyone could see it. I was flabbergasted, but as I tried to mumble my thanks he put his finger to his lips, calmly bade me adieu, and walked out of the hut.

My thoughts were in chaos, but behind them ran a bubbling spring of triumph, excitement and anticipation. I wanted to run and jump and shout for joy. I contained myself; but I had to tell someone. Ken, Ace, Nugget and Aussie were still in the hut; they all knew my plans. I drew them together.

'Well,' I said quietly, 'it's on. Definitely.'

They bombarded me with questions – how? when? – but I would only say 'soon', which drove them crazy with frustration. I felt buoyed up with confidence and an inner certainty. If I had been going out by tunnel, or by some other conventional method, I think I should have been considerably less sure of myself; but, in the mood I was in then, my way seemed to have a mad, infallible logic about it.

The other fellows, those who knew, were happy for me; we had a farewell party three nights in a row. In spite of the fact that I had told so few, the word leaked out. The authorities turned the camp upside-down, shifting the beds, testing the floors for loose boards, ripping out the stoves in their search for a tunnel, but, of course, found nothing. Meanwhile, my monk's habit remained undisturbed under my mattress, and I chuckled to myself. The failure of the Commandant to find it, or even suspect its existence, reinforced my conviction that my idea was a winner.

The following day Fra Domenico came to the camp alone; I asked him to make sure he brought Fra Filipo, who was busy elsewhere, with him the next time. Fra Domenico smiled.

'Don't be so impatient, my son. We'll both come in three days' time. And then . . .' He left the sentence unfinished. Although the final details had still to be worked out, there was no need to say any more.

Those three days were an eternity. I couldn't concentrate on anything, but wandered about the camp carrying out my duties, playing football, like an automaton. But, at last, the second evening came. I told Nugget and the others that I was going the next day. They already knew the rough outline of my plan, but the excitement and anticipation were electrifying. Strangely enough, I was the most relaxed of us all. I can't explain why.

Ace said, 'The Mad Monk strikes again,' and got a laugh. It was a change from being called The Saint, anyway. The light went out, but it was a long time before I fell asleep. Was this really my last night in Campo 303? I was sure of it, yet I couldn't believe it. I would be free tomorrow!

Chapter Three

I was awake before reveille and was dressing when the guards came in to wake us up. We went to the mess hut, but I couldn't eat. My confidence of the previous night had dissolved into a bad bout of nerves. Breakfast over, we were marched back to the hut to await our job assignment for the day. Luckily, because of the number of prisoners in the camp, there wasn't enough work for all of us, and we were given a day off.

About ten o'clock the two monks arrived, and I knew for certain it was on. Fra Domenico quickly drew me aside. Fra Filipo, he said, knew nothing of my escape. He would leave the camp, as he often did, at noon, half an hour before the gate-guard changed shifts. There was no set time of arrival or departure for the monks, who came and went as they pleased, so as long as the new shift didn't see him go, we were safe.

Twelve o'clock came, and Fra Domenico reminded Fra Filipo that he had better be going. Fra Filipo said goodbye to us and headed for the gate. The guard opened up and let him out. The relief guard was nowhere in sight; everything was going according to plan.

We went back into my hut, and while Nugget, Fra Domenico and the others crowded round my bunk, I lay on the bottom one, Nugget's, and changed into my robes. Just as I was ready, three other prisoners came in. I knew them all well, but I hadn't confided in them. Scouse caught their attention, put a finger to his lips, and drew his other hand across his throat. They realized at once what was going on, and stood staring at me, mouths agape. Fra Domenico and I passed them and strolled together out to the compound.

There was a football game in progress and we stopped and watched it for a while. I had my hood pulled over my head, but I kept my eyes peeled for any guards who might come too close.

It was now about half past one. The new shift had settled into their routine of duties at the gate. Fra Domenico touched my arm, and, accompanied by Nugget, Scouse and Ace, we left the game and set off casually towards it. I was intensely conscious that the guard was watching us. He wasn't worried about the two monks, but whenever prisoners came too close, the guards kept a sharp eye on them.

I said goodbye quickly to my shipmates, and they wished me good luck. I could sense the sadness and a certain envy in their expressions, and felt sorry, almost guilty, at leaving them behind.

Fra Domenico and I turned and walked towards the gate. The guard had already opened it by the time we got there. I walked with my head bowed as if deep in prayer – and I was praying, believe me. Fra Domenico made the sign of the Cross, murmured '*Arrivederci*' – I remember thinking 'not if I can help it!' – and we were through. The guard gave us no more than a cursory glance, and closed the gate behind us.

*

The road ran straight for about a hundred yards. We walked slowly, as if engaged in some theological debate. Fra Domenico remained perfectly calm, and though I was dying to break into a run I forced myself to keep step

27

with him. Once round the first bend we were out of sight of the gate and the machine-gun towers; we still kept walking steadily on, only a little faster now. People passing bowed to us, and I followed Fra Domenico's example and responded with the sign of the Cross.

When we had walked about three miles, he stopped.

'It is time for us to part,' he said. He gave me directions to the coast, and advice on what to do and say if I should be stopped and questioned. I could feel the tears welling up in my eyes, and I could not help embracing him. This man, a foreigner and almost a stranger, had risked his life to save mine. He embraced me in his turn, and gave me some money and his blessing. Then he turned abruptly and walked off in the direction from which we had come. I watched him until he was out of sight, and then I headed on my way.

Fra Domenico had told me that my biggest problem was not the military but the civilians. Soldiers were unlikely to speak to me, so a nod would be sufficient; but the local people would ask for my blessing, and this would inevitably lead to conversation. If I were asked where I was going, I was to say the name of the next town ahead; since there were plenty of signposts this shouldn't be difficult. When night came and I needed a place to sleep, all I had to do was go to the nearest farm and ask; they wouldn't refuse me. Fra Domenico had emphasized that I must try and avoid getting into discussions with my hosts for the night; they would offer me a meal, and after that I should make my excuses and go straight to bed. His last remark as we parted was that he would tell the boys at Campo 303 that I had made it so far, and that he believed that I should make it all the way.

Well, here I was, on the run, in a strange country knowing little of the language, and committed to posing as a man of God. I simply couldn't believe it – any of it. I felt that if I pinched myself I should wake up in the top bunk in my hut at the camp, with Nugget snoring happily away below.

Hunger and thirst brought me back to the reality of my situation; I knew that soon I should have to go to a farm and ask for food and drink, and the prospect filled me with trepidation. I walked on steadily, postponing the moment of trial as long as possible. I came to the top of a hill. In the valley below was a farmhouse surrounded by fields and outbuildings. It was suitably remote, and it lay directly on my route. This was it, then; my first contact with the population, the first, crucial, test of my disguise.

I made my way down the hill and walked boldly up to the farm. There was a boy working in the yard. He looked up as I approached and wished me '*Buona sera*'.

'*Buona sera*,' I replied. '*Ho fame e sono stanco.*'

'*Sì.*' He called towards the house. '*Mama*,' and, so far as I was able to understand it, told her they had a visitor, a *monaco*, who was tired and hungry. A woman came out of the farmhouse and asked me in. We went into the kitchen where there were two men, one in his twenties, the other, whom I assumed to be her husband, approaching middle age. As I entered they rose and greeted me, and invited me to join them at the table. I sat down and held my crucifix in front of me as if I were meditating, but I'm afraid my thoughts were more on the delicious smell of cooking.

The woman put the food on the table, and everyone sat down. I suddenly realized they were waiting for me to say grace. I murmured something appropriate; the older man said '*Buon appetito*' and poured wine into our glasses, while his wife served the meal. There was not much conversation, just a few words among themselves, mostly about the food. This suited me admirably.

When we had finished eating I remarked casually that I had walked a long way that day and would be glad to go

29

to bed. There was no spare room in the house, the farmer said; but if I wouldn't mind sleeping in the barn, I was very welcome. I assured them I didn't mind in the least, whereupon the boy fetched a blanket, and led the way.

He wished me '*Buona notte*', and left me. For a time I strolled round the yard, making a note of the layout in case I had to leave in a hurry. I had come a few miles that day, but it might not be enough if my disguise had become known at Campo 303 and the word had been put about. The further I was from Pavia, the safer I should be. One thing, however, was perfectly genuine: I was dog-tired. In a mood that was a blend of triumph, excitement, anxiety and exhaustion, I finally went into the barn, lay down in the hay, covered myself with the blanket and fell asleep almost immediately.

*

I was woken by the boy early the next morning. He babbled something from which I recognized the word '*il caffè*'. I got up, washed at the fountain in the yard and went into the house. The family were already seated at the table; the older man waved me to a seat. Again I said grace, and we wished each other '*Buon appetito*'. Breakfast consisted of home-baked bread and strong coffee. The family talked among themselves, and I behaved as though I was deep in thought – as indeed I was, trying to plan my next move. When we had finished the meal, I said I must be on my way. The farmer's wife gave me a package containing salami, cheese and bread; I thanked her as profusely as my limited Italian would allow, and as I made to move, the farmer told the boy to accompany me a little way and put me on the right road. They hadn't asked me where I was going, and I hadn't told them.

The boy came with me for about a mile. When we parted, I asked him the way to the next town. He pointed in the general direction, saying that it was about 25 kilometres off, wished me '*Buona fortuna*' and set off back to the farm.

The sun was getting hot by this time and I didn't try to rush. I reckoned I had five hours' hard walking ahead of me, and a steady pace would be better than fast bursts interspersed with rests. I also decided not to talk to anyone, unless it was absolutely necessary; I wasn't ready for conversation yet, and to attempt it with my halting Italian seemed a pointless risk. Even avoiding casual contact as much as possible, I wondered how long I could get away with it. I had only been gone from the camp one night, but it seemed a year.

I worried about whether, when my escape had been discovered, there had been any reprisals. The evening roll-call would show I was missing; but I had left no clues; no tunnel, no cut wire, nothing. I was sure that the few people who knew how I had escaped would not say anything; and for just so long as the authorities didn't know of my disguise, I had a good chance of getting away with it. Assuming that they didn't know it, they wouldn't know what to look for or where to begin; but, on the other hand, if they *did* know, they only had to stop every monk within a fifty-mile radius of Campo 303 and they would be sure to catch me. Moreover, I had no means of knowing in advance, and so, perhaps, of stealing some civilian clothes and changing my appearance. It was in the lap of the gods. On balance, I reckoned my chances were about 50/50. With this fairly encouraging thought, I plodded on my way.

I hadn't gone very far when a convoy of military trucks approached from ahead. My first instinct was to make myself scarce, but there wasn't enough cover to hide a rabbit – nothing but fields stretching away for miles. The only thing to do was to keep walking and try to appear unconcerned when I came abreast of them. As they drew nearer, I was relieved to see that they were Italian. There were four of them; and in the open back of each there were soldiers who were singing.

As they passed me they all waved and shouted, '*Buon giorno, Padre.*' I waved back in pure relief. Italian soldiers seemed so lax and easy-going that, although I had no intention of underestimating them, I felt that it wouldn't be too difficult to fool them. The Germans, I was sure, and as Fra Domenico had said, were a very different matter.

Chapter Four

I HAD been walking now for three days, lying up at night in shepherds' huts. Apart from the fact that I still had no clear plan of action, and didn't really know where I was, everything, so far, had gone well. I stopped at the side of the road for a bite to eat, and saw a uniformed figure approaching on a bicycle. By the shape of his hat I knew he was a *carabiniere*, and I was on my guard at once. He slowed down and dismounted beside me.

'*Buon giorno, Padre.*'

'*Buon giorno,*' I replied, hoping he wasn't feeling inclined for a chat.

'*Fa caldo,*' he remarked, mopping his brow. It certainly was hot, and I probably felt a lot hotter than he did. To make conversation, I asked him how far it was to the next city.

'It is forty kilometres to Alessandria,' he said, 'but the village of Arpi is only six kilometres.'

I thanked him and said that I must be moving on. I could have done with a longer rest, but I felt uneasy and vulnerable in his presence. I didn't know if he was a danger to me, and I didn't mean to find out.

He got back on his bicycle, and after wishing me '*Arrivederci*', pushed off; and I continued walking in the direction of Alessandria.

*

My lack of fluent Italian was my main anxiety in those

first few days, and I spent a lot of time and mental energy trying to think of an explanation that would sound plausible if I was questioned. Could I describe myself as an American student monk, I wondered? But America was already in the war, so that wouldn't wash. I should still be a belligerent. Though I didn't know it then, the perfect solution was waiting just round the corner of my mind, and it popped out during my next encounter.

This was with a farmer trundling along the road in a cart. I must have been day-dreaming, for the sound of the horse's hooves quite startled me. As it drew level, I waved to the driver, and he reined in and stopped.

'Are you going in the direction of Arpi?' I asked.

He nodded and told me to climb aboard; then he shook the reins, and the horse started off again at a slow trot. As we jogged along, he glanced at me.

'You're tired, Padre?'

I nodded. 'And hungry!' I didn't understand his next question: it obviously was a question because he sat looking at me as if waiting for an answer. I asked him to repeat it, and he said, '*E italiano?*'

'No,' I replied, and, without thinking, added, '*Io sono irlandese.*' Why I picked Ireland as my homeland I can't imagine; but I couldn't have made a luckier choice. Eire was Catholic; she was neutral; and there was nothing odd about an Irish monk, speaking broken Italian, wandering the roads of wartime Italy. The farmer certainly appeared to see nothing strange about it.

'Are you going far?'

'To Alessandria.'

'It will take you a few days' walking,' he said. 'You will be welcome to spend the night at my house, if you wish.'

I accepted gratefully, and we continued our jogging progress through the flat countryside.

The farm, when we finally reached it, was not as secluded

34

as I would have liked, and it bore the appearance of having come down in the world. I reckoned they must have been hard put to eke a living from it. Yet, as we went into the house, the familiar smell of cooking filled my nostrils. No matter how poor they were, these people were always cooking. I could have eaten an elephant, but I tried not to show it in case they started to question me.

I was introduced to the members of the Ferraro family who were present, and offered a glass of wine. I asked if I could have some milk instead, and was given a large glass. I wanted to drain it at a gulp, but remembered my role and sipped it with what I felt was becoming restraint.

One of their sons was in the army, and his three children, as well as the children of a daughter, whose husband was working in the fields, were living at the farm. I was shown photographs of the soldier son, and also some faded ones of Papa Luigi as an Alpini in the 1914–18 War.

The others started drifting into the house from their work, and I was introduced to them. When everyone was present we all sat down at the large table. I was given the seat to the right of Papa, the place of the guest of honour. During dinner I was bombarded with questions; what was I doing in Italy? where was I going? why was I going there? I told them that I was a novice, and that I was making my way to Rome to continue my studies. This must have sounded convincing, because the talk turned to other subjects.

When we had finished, Papa asked me if I had any objection to their smoking.

'I don't mind,' I said, but I didn't join them. The tobacco they used was foul; it smelled like manure.

While the women cleared away the dishes and set to washing up, the men sat at the table smoking. I was asked about Ireland, and how it compared with Italy, and answered as best I could. Very little was said about the war, other than that they wished it was over and their family

35

reunited. Papa asked me why I had chosen my vocation as a monk, and I said that the Irish, like the Italians, were much inclined towards the Church. This went over well; and I blessed the inspiration that had caused me to choose my nationality.

After another hour or so of small talk, I asked them to excuse me, as I was tired, having walked many miles that day. One of the younger boys had been made to give up his bed for me, and after many *buona notte*'s all round, I went up to the room I had been shown earlier. I had thought that I would fall asleep immediately; but I hovered on the brink of consciousness for a long time. I thought back over my travels, of all that had happened since I escaped and of the camp itself and the friends I had left there. I hoped nobody had suffered because of me. I also thought about the future. What was in store for me during the weeks ahead? On that unprofitable speculation I finally fell asleep.

*

I awoke with a start the following morning. The first thing I was aware of was the pain in my feet. The continuous walking in the rough sandals which Fra Domenico had given me had left them cut and swollen. The next thing was the wound in my arm, which I'd neglected, and which was beginning to bother me again.

Downstairs, the others were already having breakfast. Papa noticed me limping and looked at my feet. He shook his head.

'*Molto doloroso,*' he said. 'You must stay here until they're better.'

I was still uneasy about staying long in one place, but I really had no alternative.

'Make yourself at home, and rest,' said Papa as he and the other men left for the fields, so I spent a lazy day bathing my feet and trying to plan my next move.

Up to now I had had no clear idea of where to make for; I was more concerned with putting the greatest possible distance between me and the camp. Fra Domenico had set me on the road to 'the coast'; but I had no map, and only the haziest picture of the geography of Italy, and I wasn't even sure which coast he had meant. And what was I supposed to do, if and when I reached it? Ideally, I should have been trying to make contact with Allied troops; but I hadn't heard how the war was going nor where the Allies were since my escape. As far as I knew, the nearest were in Egypt or Gibraltar.

On Fra Domenico's advice, I had been heading approximately south-west since leaving the camp, roughly in the direction of Genoa. I had toyed with the idea of turning round and making for Switzerland, but even I realized that I would not only have to cross the Alps, but also risk finding myself in one of the large northern cities, Turin or Milan, which would certainly be full of German troops. And the Italo-Swiss frontier would inevitably be heavily guarded. I wanted to avoid the Germans at all costs, because I knew that the Gestapo would have detachments in the larger cities, and even if I were caught by the Wehrmacht, they would turn me over to the Gestapo. My disguise would be considered civilian attire, and there was an even chance I should be shot as a spy.

If, on the other hand, I kept going until I reached the coast, I had two possible alternatives. I might either be able to work my way west, through unoccupied France to Spain – the refuge of innumerable escaped prisoners – or I could keep going south along the coast until I reached the toe of Italy. There, or in Sicily if I could cross the Straits of Messina, I might be able to steal a boat and get across to North Africa. Either route would be a long haul, and I could have no idea what I should find at the end – if, that is, I made it. Time enough to worry about that; at least now I had a clearer picture of my next move. And one thing was certain, I couldn't get far with my feet – or my arm – in their present condition. The first and most important thing was to get fit, even if it meant staying on at the farm. If my disguise had been discovered at the camp I only hoped that none of the members of this family would idly mention to anyone in the village of Arpi that they had an 'Irish monk' staying with them.

*

In the end I spent just over a fortnight there. I was with the children most of the time, and this did wonders for my Italian. I may have been taking a chance, because the children picked up a few English words; but it seemed a small risk when my whole existence was so precarious, and worth it for the rewards. The local school, I discovered, was two miles from the farm, and the teachers were nuns. I stowed this information away for future reference; it might be useful in an emergency, for I was sure that nuns wouldn't give me away.

Guglielmo, one of the farm hands, took a great liking to me. At 16, he was too old for school, and too young for the army; a charming, intelligent lad, who felt, perhaps, confined by farm life, and was ready to fall under the spell of a foreigner. I would have liked to tell him the truth about myself, for I felt uncomfortable about deceiving him; but caution prevailed. Much as I liked him and enjoyed his friendship, I had too much to lose. I realized subconsciously that, although I had escaped very ill-prepared for what was to come, I was quickly learning the elementary lessons of self-preservation.

When I was able to walk around without pain I asked Guglielmo the way to the school. He said he would take me there himself. On the way I showed him my bandaged arm, and made gestures to indicate a gun. He nodded, showing that he understood. I removed the bandages, and when he saw the open wound, I thought he would throw up.

'*Che male, molto male,*' he exclaimed, quite pale, 'we'd better go back.'

'No,' I said, '*per la scuola.*' He shrugged and we carried on. After a silence, he asked:

'Who shot you?'

I hesitated; but in this case the truth was safe. I made motions with my hands to indicate a plane, and imitated a machine-gun.

'*Tedeschi,*' I said, 'the Germans.' He didn't question me any further.

Once at the school, we were greeted by the Head Sister, Sister Saveria. Guglielmo introduced us, and then he and she had a long conversation; finally she led us to a room off the main hall, and asked to see my arm. She examined the wound, then said something to Guglielmo, who disappeared. But he was soon back with bandages and a bottle of some lotion, and accompanied by a nun carrying a bowl of water. She and the Sister bathed my arm and anointed it with the lotion; I don't know what was in that bottle but it certainly did the trick: I passed out cold!

For the next two or three days I was in high fever and delirious, nursed by Sister Saveria and the nuns. At some point I must have rambled on in English – one of my most potent terrors – for Sister Saveria told me afterwards that she knew my nationality, though she asked no questions. I only prayed that my delirious outbursts had been in keeping with my calling – or that she hadn't understood them! The nuns were kindness itself during the remainder of my stay at the farm; through their treatment, the wound finally healed; and when I left, they presented me with a satchel for my food and small possessions.

The people at the farm were genuinely happy to see me recovering. Inevitably, they asked me why my arm was in a sling. I shrugged it off, saying that it was only a scratch which had become infected. I looked at Guglielmo as I said this, and he gave a slight nod, just to let me know that I could trust him not to say any more. Only one of the family, Angelo, kept on asking questions about it. It was only natural inquisitiveness, but I wasn't taking any chances; and pretended not to understand.

After dinner on my last night on the farm, Guglielmo told me that he wanted to leave with me, and would like to take me to the home of his family in Saluzzo. It was quite a surprise, and I had to think fast. If I refused I would have to offer a reason, and, other than the truth, I couldn't think of one. On the other hand, it would be useful to have a companion. So I accepted with pleasure.

The following morning, Guglielmo and I set off. In some ways I was sorry to go; but from the point of view of the safety of the people who had shown me so much kindness, as well as my own, it was unwise to linger. I should never forget the children – Pino, Alda, Pepe, Gina and Maria – with whom I had spent so much time, and from whom I had learnt a considerable amount of Italian. They never asked the awkward questions which adults have a way of doing, and in their company I was able to relax. I could have hugged them all when we said goodbye, but I wasn't sure whether such emotion went with the dignity of my robes, so I restrained myself.

The farmer's wife gave us food to take with us; even with the war, I noticed, the farmers didn't go short and there was plenty to spare. As we waved goodbye, I had a tremendous feeling of well-being. I was fit again, and any fears that my escape hadn't been worth it had vanished. Whatever the future held, these three weeks of freedom had been a tonic which I wouldn't have missed for the world. And with each day that I stayed free, my confidence increased.

Chapter Five

AFTER about three hours of steady walking we came to the first signpost; it showed direction and distance to Turin, Alessandria, Novara, Saluzzo and Cuneo. I wanted to memorize these names, so I suggested to Guglielmo that we should rest there and eat. He agreed, and while we lunched, I asked him about the places on the signpost. Turin, I knew, was a large industrial city, which I intended to avoid. Apart from the Gestapo, I expected that there might well be other monks there, and a meeting with them might be awkward since I shouldn't know what questions they would ask me nor how I should answer them. So I concentrated on Saluzzo and Cuneo. Guglielmo told me that both places were to the south-west of us, above the Italian Riviera. This sounded more promising, I thought; but I didn't know then that the Germans were using that coast as rest bases for their troops.

By the time we moved on there was quite a bit of traffic on the road, mostly army trucks, and after a mile or so I had my first encounter with the Germans. I saw their truck coming, and knew that if they stopped Guglielmo, I should have to stop too. I didn't understand any German, and I didn't want to say I was Irish in case of complications, so pointing to myself I said to Guglielmo:

'Don't tell them I'm Irish.'

He nodded, and then, as I was afraid it would, the German truck stopped. One of the soldiers in the cab called to Guglielmo, who walked over to him; they spoke for a moment, and then he produced his papers. The German examined them, handed them back, and gestured towards me. Guglielmo said something I didn't catch, and the soldier made a motion like a salute in my direction. I raised my hand in acknowledgement and walked slowly ahead, expecting, at any second, an abrupt and guttural command to 'Halt!' The other occupants of the truck were talking among themselves, and, as when Fra Domenico and I had strolled away from the camp, I forced myself not to hurry, not to look round. At last, an order was given and the truck pulled away. The palms of my hands were wet with sweat.

Guglielmo fell in step with me and told me what had happened. He had been asked for his identity papers, which was normal; then he had been asked about me. He had told them that I was on my way to a monastery in Piedmonte, and after some hesitation, they'd accepted it. I didn't know where Piedmonte was, nor, indeed, if there was a monastery there; but if Germans believed the story, it must at least be plausible, so I tucked it away in my mind for future reference.

As the day wore on, the traffic on the road increased until it was a continuous stream of military vehicles. According to Guglielmo, they were bound for Genoa and Savona, which were two of the main embarkation points for German soldiers and equipment bound for the Middle East. They seemed to be making no secret of their movements, probably because the war was going in their favour. I made a note to steer clear of Genoa and Savona; but it occurred to me that I was in a unique position to damage the Axis war machine, if only I knew how to set about it. As it was, I was helpless.

*

We arrived at the home of Guglielmo's parents just as the sun was going down. Their farm lay in a valley sheltered by the Maritime Alps, a very picturesque spot. Guglielmo introduced me to his family. He'd been away for almost a year, and they made a great fuss of him. There were Mama and Papa, whose christian names were Amelia and Ferruccio; they made me welcome and told me that their house was mine for as long as I wished. Then there were Guglielmo's brothers and sisters – Assunta 20, Maria 18, Angelina 17, Rodolfo 15, Erminio 12 and the youngest, Giulio, who was five. In addition there were Donnatella, the general help, and Giovanni Bossi, who was *nonno*, the grandfather. It seemed that all the older men of this region of Italy had fought in the Alpini in the 1914–18 War, and Grandfather Bossi was no exception. He told me all about it, and showed me the faded photographs of himself in uniform, and the medals he had won.

Guglielmo was the eldest son, so his homecoming was just cause for a celebration. Rodolfo and Erminio were at once sent out to spread the good news to friends and relatives in the vicinity, and in less than an hour they began to arrive – cousins, uncles, aunts, about thirty in all. The table was set, the food brought out; I said grace, the wine was poured. What a meal! It was nothing short of magnificent. Everyone was in high spirits, and even though I still couldn't join in the conversation, I was given a running commentary by Guglielmo, who was seated next to me. No one mentioned the war, although there was a blackout, and once in a while I heard what sounded like heavy bombers flying overhead. Guglielmo told me that they were most likely bombing Turin or other cities in that area, but I didn't hear any anti-aircraft fire, which struck me as peculiar.

I ate a lot, but took care not to drink too much of the potent, home-made wine. *Nonno* Bossi drank my share as well as his own, and with each glass, got louder and more jovial. He eventually commandeered the conversation, no mean feat at a table of thirty Italians, all drinking and

43

celebrating. He must have been a born comedian because every sentence was greeted with roars of laughter from the others. Once or twice I heard him say the word *Tedeschi*, after which everyone laughed. Guglielmo translated one particular sally as being that whenever German soldiers came to the Bossi farm for food, there was never any there, and yet here we sat with enough to feed a regiment. Even with everyone laughing at the Germans, I wasn't absolutely sure which way their sympathies lay; it was clear that they resented their being in Italy, but my feeling was that they were prepared to put up with them rather than actively oppose them.

While the merriment was going on, I found my attention drawn more and more towards Assunta, the eldest girl. She had a shy, untouched beauty that really stirred me, and I couldn't keep my eyes off her, although I knew it was out of character. It was a long time since I had been close to a pretty girl, without barbed wire between us. I learned that she was unattached, and that her mother was afraid she would remain so, because all the eligible men were away at the war. I could hardly tell her that, in my own eyes at least, I was eligible.

I excused myself from the table and went outside for some air. There was no moon, but the stars, reflecting on the Alpine snows, bathed the valley in an eerie glow. It had been warm in the house, and the coolness of the night air made me aware of the strength of the wine I had drunk.

After a few minutes, I was joined by Guglielmo, his father, and an uncle, Arturo Franchi. They were in good spirits and asked me if I felt all right. Arturo jokingly suggested I might have had too much vino, at which Guglielmo admonished him for saying such a thing to a man of the cloth. It made me realize how good my disguise really was. The *carabinieri*, the German soldier, the nuns and now Guglielmo, were all completely convinced that I was exactly what I appeared to be. Could I keep it up, and for how long? Charming creatures like Assunta didn't help.

To get out of Italy, through France, and into Spain, I knew I should need allies. Could I gain the confidence of these genial people so that I could divulge my true identity? First, I would have to be certain of their feelings concerning the war, and to do that, I should have to stay with them for a while. My friendship with Guglielmo had immediately made me accepted – but as a monk, not as an escaped British PoW. I decided to wait until the following day before making up my mind.

We were joined by Ettore, another uncle. He was a very big man, and with his weather-beaten complexion looked the complete farmer; yet I sensed as underlying force which suggested he might have another less rustic side. He spoke to me in Italian, but I didn't understand what he said. Guglielmo explained that I was Irish and had been studying in Italy. Ettore suddenly beamed.

'Before the war,' he said in English, 'I have worked in a large hotel in Switzerland, so I speak a little.'

I felt at once that I was in luck. There was something about Ettore, an integrity, which inspired a sense of trust; but, in spite of this, I was wary. How did I know where his loyalties lay? Nevertheless, he immediately became the self-appointed link between the others and myself.

It was getting late now and the guests had started to drift home. I was to share Guglielmo's room, which had been converted from a loft over the stables into a very comfortable bedroom. The house itself was spotless, but the amenities were, to say the least, antiquated. There was no sewage system, just a ditch in a field into which everything was dumped. When the ditch was full, they simply dug another one. Guglielmo told me that there was a government levy on livestock and farmers could only own so many sheep, goats, pigs and so on; any over the permitted number

45

would be confiscated. This was more of an inconvenience than a hardship, and although I'd heard stories of food shortages in Italy, I hadn't seen any evidence of them. Of course, I hadn't been in any big towns, where, Guglielmo told me, things were much worse than in the country. Clothing and food were both rationed; but again country people didn't feel this as much as townsfolk.

Lying in bed that night, and trying to look ahead, it seemed to me that I had better stick to the country, where food was more plentiful and the people were less suspicious. That had been my experience so far, and I had no reason to think it would be different in other parts of Italy. I thought how lucky I'd been – and then I thought of Assunta, and forgot about plots and plans. I was still thinking about her when I fell asleep.

Chapter Six

I COULDN'T get that girl out of my mind. She and I had exchanged glances across the table many times in the past three days: was she intrigued by me because I was a monk, or in spite of it? After dinner each evening I had made it my habit to stroll around outside to make my plans undisturbed. On this, the third evening, I was sauntering up and down as usual when I heard the door of the house open and close. I had my back to it, and turned too late to see who had come out. Footsteps approached, light, dainty, not a man's, I thought.

'*Fra Giuseppe!*' It was Assunta.

'*Si, Signorina?*' I answered.

She came very close to me.

'It is so hot indoors,' she said.

We stood in silence for a few moments, and then she took my hand. I could feel the contours of her body, her small, firm breasts, pressing against me. It was more than flesh and blood could stand after the weeks of enforced celibacy. I took her in my arms, and she returned my kisses with an equal passion. Half-stumbling, we moved together away from the house, where the leafy trees cast deep shadows and hid the stars.

'Assunta!' I murmured; and when we lay together on the brittle ground she made no resistance, but twined herself around me as if her need was as desperate as my own.

It was a precious moment, even if I was uneasily aware of the door, and her no doubt jealously possessive family on the

47

far side of it. As long as they stayed there. . . . At last we forced ourselves to get up and go indoors. No one showed the least concern at our absence, and after a little while I excused myself and went off to bed. But it was a long time before I got to sleep. In one way, I was appalled at my own rashness, but at the same time, I felt enraptured.

Up to now, the longing for freedom, on my own terms, had been my driving force. It still was; but after this experience with Assunta, it had become complicated by other factors. I knew I would continue to meet her whenever possible, so I didn't want to leave the Bossi's; on the other hand, if I stayed too long, somebody might get curious. Should I tell them the truth? To give up my disguise would be foolish because, dressed as a civilian, I would need papers and a full command of the Italian language, and I had neither. I didn't like deceiving the Bossi's, and at the same time, I didn't want to compromise them. They were such good people, involved in this war without their wish, and by circumstances beyond their control.

If I was going to confide in anyone, it would have to be Guglielmo, or, perhaps, Ettore. It was a difficult decision, and needed much thought. And there was another thing – supposing Assunta became pregnant? She would be disgraced in her parents' eyes, and I would forfeit any respect they might have had for me, as a man, and as a monk. Perhaps if I told them the truth, things would be better. How would they react? They were in as much danger as I was myself, for the Germans imposed fearful reprisals on those who helped escaped prisoners. Yet I terribly wanted to stay, because of Assunta. I was deeply in love with her; and for the time being that over-shadowed all other considerations. At last, after much tossing and turning, I made up my mind to ask Ferruccio Bossi if I could stay on for a little longer.

I broached the subject at breakfast next day. He said I

could stay as long as I liked, but when I pressed him to let me help with the farm work, he wouldn't hear of it at first. I insisted, and after a lot of persuasion, he agreed.

I would have liked to dispense with my habit, but I still didn't dare; soldiers sometimes came to the farm, and I was much safer as Fra Giuseppe. On the whole, the Italian soldiers were respectful to civilians, though very easy-going among themselves. They would always accept some wine and flirt with the girls. Luckily it never went further than that, because I swear that if one of them had laid a hand on Assunta, I would have broken his neck.

One afternoon, though, a German staff car came to the farm. In it were a number of German and Italian officers and NCOs, which was odd, as they rarely mixed except at high command levels. This party was looking for billets for German officers. Ferruccio told them that there was only room for one, but that they might have better luck with the other farmers in the area. The Italians translated, and they conferred together for a few minutes. Then the Italian officer thanked Ferruccio and saluted, and they all got back into the car and left.

The indications were that the Germans were building up their forces in this district. Why else should they need quarters for their officers? The implications, for me, were both alarming and depressing, for it meant that I should have to leave the Bossi's. I should have to plan a route, think up a suitable excuse to satisfy the family, and especially Assunta, and get away as fast as possible.

I broke the news at dinner that evening. They all expressed their regrets, but respected my decision. As it happened, Ettore was there, and when we had finished eating, he, Guglielmo and I went out into the yard. I told them that my real reason for leaving was because of the Germans moving into the area.

'I don't blame you,' Ettore said, 'I do not like the Germans

49

either; and, between you and me, I do not love Mussolini or his Fascisti.'

I tried not to show too much interest in his views, yet I felt that he was probing me, feeling me out. Did he suspect that I was not what I seemed? Would it be wise to trust him? I couldn't be sure.

After a while, he went back into the house and I decided there was nothing for it but to tell Guglielmo everything.

When I had finished, he just sat stunned for a time; then he started laughing. He congratulated me on my escape and said he would like to have seen it all, from the time I walked out of Campo 303 with Fra Domenico. Then, more seriously, he assured me that I need have no fear of his family and their friends. He agreed that it would be better if I moved on, but recommended me to make for Sicily rather than Spain. France, even the Vichy south, which was technically un-occupied, would be more dangerous for me than Italy, and he promised to plan a route which would keep me away from military areas, and also well away from Campo 303.

I had told Guglielmo everything about myself – except my affair with Assunta – and that same evening I took her out-side and repeated the whole story to her. When she realized that I wasn't really a monk at all, she broke down and cried, mainly from relief, I think, because her sin was less dreadful than she had supposed.

Now that my secret was out, the parting would be more difficult than ever. I told Guglielmo about his sister and myself; he didn't seem surprised, but I hadn't gone into de-tails, simply told him how we felt about each other. He em-braced me, and said it was a pity there was a war on, and that he knew his parents would be happy with the news; and indeed, when I finally told them, not only about my true identity but about Assunta and me, they were a little be-wildered at first, but only for a moment or two. As soon as it had sunk in, I was embraced, hugged and kissed by the whole family. Ettore clapped me on the back, almost knocking me down, and shook my hand furiously.

'I wish I were in your shoes, Giuseppe. I'd show the *sporchi Tedeschi*—filthy Boche—and the *sporchi Fascisti* what I thought of them!'

He volunteered to accompany me as far south as he could, at least until I was well away from any German units.

The children, quite baffled by all the excitement, quickly caught the mood, and went dashing around, laughing and shouting. Mama Bossi was overjoyed; I was the answer to her prayers for Assunta, she exclaimed. How it would all work out, only the Good Lord could tell, and she crossed herself fervently.

Ferruccio brought out the wine, and this time I didn't have to watch my cloth. I drank glass for glass with all of them, Ferruccio, Ettore, Guglielmo and grandfather Giovanni. The relief at appearing before them in my true colours combined with the wine to make me feel happier than I had for a long time. Even the thought of the parting – particularly from Assunta who had given herself to me in that first passionate moment – wasn't enough to cloud the atmosphere of spontaneous rejoicing.

The following morning I was roused by little Giulio – some Germans were coming up the road to the farm. I dressed hurriedly, went into the kitchen, and sat at the table next to Giovanni Bossi. Ettore, Guglielmo and the younger children were there, while Mama and Assunta were busy about their normal household chores. Assunta looked worried, and inwardly so was I; but the weeks of posing as a monk had given me an outward calm which came naturally to me now, and enabled me to hide my true feelings.

Assunta brought me some coffee, bread and salami – my last meal, I thought. It could very well be, if the Germans found out who I really was. Then came the sound I had been dreading, a heavy pounding on the front door. I bowed my

51

head as if in prayer, and grandfather Bossi opened the door. A German lieutenant, accompanied by a sergeant, walked in. The lieutenant looked around the room and said something in German to Giovanni.

'*Non capisco, Tedescho,*' the old man replied.

'Who are you?' the sergeant asked him in Italian.

'My son owns this farm,' Giovanni replied.

The sergeant passed this information on to the lieutenant who pointed to the rest of us and said something in German.

'And the others?' the sergeant asked.

Giovanni explained, adding that I had simply stayed there overnight. This wasn't good enough for the lieutenant, he wanted to know where I had come from, where I was going, and why. I was on my way, I said, from Turin to Rome, to complete my studies. This seemed to satisfy him.

They were still looking for quarters for their officers; but when Giovanni told him that they had already been asked, and could only put up one man, the lieutenant retorted that if they had been able to put me up, they could certainly accommodate others, and demanded to see where I had slept. On that evidence, he said that there was room for four NCOs, and that they would be moving in that same afternoon. I could see why most of the Italian civilians were unsympathetic towards the Germans.

Ferruccio came back at that moment. He was reluctant to accept the German's terms, but what could he do? It was all settled. The two snapped their heels and walked out. As soon as they were safely out of the way, I told Guglielmo I would have to leave before the lodgers arrived. Ferruccio agreed, and when Guglielmo asked if he could come with me, he shrugged and said 'If you like'. In a few months Guglielmo was due to be conscripted into the Italian army.

While Ettore planned our route, Mama Bossi prepared food for us to take. My thoughts were on Assunta. I could hardly bear to think of her with four German soldiers in the house.

When the time came for us to leave, she was in tears. She pleaded to be allowed to come with us. I knew she was concerned in case she was pregnant; if I had known for certain that she was, I would most likely have stayed. But as far as either of us knew, she wasn't. I was torn between my feelings for her and my instinct to be as far away from the farm as possible before the Germans moved in. The instinct for self-preservation was uppermost.

Mama Bossi gave us the food she had prepared, and embraced us all; Ferruccio embraced me and wished me '*buona fortuna*'; grandfather Bossi shook my hand warmly.

'I wish I were younger and could come with you,' he said. Finally we went out into the yard and set off. I tried hard not to look back, but my will wasn't strong enough. Assunta was not with the others waving goodbye, thank God, because I'm sure if she had been I would have run back and stayed.

Chapter Seven

ETTORE had planned our route so that we would travel through farm country all the way. We should go south to Rapallo, by-passing Genoa, on past Pisa to Grosseto; miss Rome and turn inland to Frascati, and make our way across to Bari on the Adriatic coast. From there we would follow the coast to Brindisi, go along the Gulf of Taranto into the province of Calabria, and down to the toe of the boot, Reggio di Calabria, from where, Ettore said, I could easily cross the Straits of Messina into Sicily, where I should be able to get across to North Africa. He made it sound delightfully easy.

The country was beautiful; it seemed heart-breaking that man had to ruin it with his war machines. There was plenty of traffic on the road, the majority of it heading south for Genoa; convoys of trucks full of troops, supply trucks, ammunition trucks and tankers in a continuous stream. I suddenly had a crazy idea. Instead of by-passing Genoa, perhaps I could go into the city and stow away on one of the troop transports heading for the Middle East. But I quickly rejected it. I had been lucky so far, but to have succeeded with this scheme, I would have needed a miracle, not luck.

I didn't sleep too well on our first night out, for now that I was away from the comparative security of the four walls of the Bossi farm, all my fears returned. I found I had begun to take the Italians for granted; their soldiers were so easy-going, it was difficult not to be lulled into a false sense of security. They so obviously accepted me as a monk; and all that day, as the trucks passed us, they waved to me. The Germans, on the other hand, merely gave us suspicious glances. I wondered what would have happened if I had tried to pass as a civilian; I would probably have been drafted into the Italian army!

It was now more than six weeks since I had escaped. I thought of Fra Domenico: what was he doing? Was he safe? Had my method of escape been discovered? If it had, he was certainly in serious trouble, possibly dead. Yet I was sure that he had been praying for me, because somebody was watching over me. Ettore and Guglielmo were both in good spirits, and I was glad of their companionship. Without them, my anxieties would have been unbearable.

The sun was hot, and during one of our halts the effect of it, and of the wine, made me very talkative. After a time, Ettore remarked that my Italian was getting really good; it was certainly true that I had made rapid progress, although my vocabulary was still not very extensive. The compliment did a lot for my confidence. I was also learning the basics of astro-navigation. I knew most of the major stars and the main constellations, which could be very useful if I ever had to move alone at night.

The weather was excellent, as the rainy season was still some two months away, and we were getting along well. We came to Ovada and found it was market day. The square was crowded with people, among them a number of monks. I had always been a bit nervous about meeting others of my own calling, and, without making it too obvious, we steered clear of them. I managed to keep them in view through the crowd and watched their actions carefully. I noted the way they kept fingering their rosaries, and, to my surprise, saw one of them bring out a purse. I had imagined that monks were forbidden to carry money, and had taken care not to reveal the little I had; apparently I was being over-cautious. Later, when I had seen monks and priests drinking and wenching like other men, I realized that I credited the cloth with more virtue than it deserved, and became less careful of my own behaviour. But as I watched those monks in Ovada, I felt like an actor learning a part – which was just what I was.

There were plenty of German and Italian soldiers about, but they didn't bother us. It seemed that everyone was off-duty on market day. Everyone except me, that is. In my role I couldn't relax for a second. We bought cheese, bread and sausage at one of the grocery stalls, and Ettore went to a cantina and bought some vino. He and Guglielmo paid for everything but I resolved that some day, somehow, I would pay them back.

We spent the night at the inevitable farm, in the loft over the cattle shed – which smelt powerfully – and shared the inevitable evening meal with the farmer and his family. The inevitable vino was brought out and passed around, followed by salami, cheese, bread and spaghetti. Though pasta, in its many forms, was certainly the staple of the Italian diet, salami, cheese and bread ran it a close second. Inevitably, before anyone started, I said grace and then wished everyone '*Buon appetito*'. The reply came back, '*Altro tanto*'. '*Altro tanto*' I repeated, and we fell to. The routine varied no more than did the questioning which formed the basis of every casual conversation. I knew the answers by heart now. Yet neither the act of saying grace, nor the small talk, would ever become entirely a matter of routine. The successful actor never forgets for a moment the character he is supposed to be.

This was a small family, with two sons in the army, two younger ones of six and four, and a daughter of twelve. The youngsters, as always, made friends quickly, and as soon as they had finished eating, they were chatting away to Guglielmo. Then they started to play soldiers – with the English as the enemy!

On the walls were photographs of Mussolini with his permanent scowl, and posters proclaiming *'Viva Mussolini'* and *'Viva il Duce'*; he and his henchmen, Ciano and the rest, all looked, in their braided, bemedalled uniforms, as if they had stepped out of the chorus of an opera.

Ettore and I had discussed the war while we had been walking. He didn't like the Germans as they were too militaristic, and he wasn't convinced that Italy had been right to ally herself with them. On the other hand, he resented Britain's sanctions against Italy during her war with Abyssinia; the Italians, he maintained, had civilized the country, and should have been left alone. As he had fought there, I supposed he knew what he was talking about. I personally felt that Italy should have kept out of the present war altogether, just as Switzerland had, and he agreed; adding that as long as the war didn't directly affect him or his family, he didn't really care which way it went. All he wanted was to be able to return to his farm and take up his life where he had been forced to leave it. This attitude was general among the country folk I met, and I could sympathize with it. At heart, most people involved with the war felt the same.

Next morning we were woken by the children, and after breakfast Ettore and Guglielmo helped with some ploughing as a token of our gratitude. I offered to help too, but was politely refused, so, instead, I talked to the children while the others went to work. When Ettore and Guglielmo returned to the house, we set off again.

After a time we came to a main road with a signpost pointing to Rapallo to the south-east. It, too, was thronged with military traffic, heading most likely, so Ettore said, for the Italian naval base at Leghorn. I would have given my right arm to have been able to halt their progress somehow;

but how? This was really no time for heroics, and I had had no training in sabotage. I didn't even know where the Allies were, nor had I any method of contacting them. Yet, all round me, was information that might well be of considerable value to the Allied cause.

One of the trucks pulled out of a convoy and the driver offered us a lift. It was quite a relief; we were expecting to be asked for papers; and we accepted, not least because it might have seemed suspicious not to. We climbed into the back of the truck and the soldiers made room for us. They all seemed very happy and friendly, and plied us with questions about the various districts in which they lived. From their conversation we learned that they were indeed going to Leghorn; Ettore had been right. Moreover, they were all wearing the khaki desert battle-dress of the Italian army, so they were obviously bound for North Africa. From what I could learn from them, the Germans appeared to be in complete command there.

Just then a staff car overtook us. It had swastikas painted on the doors, and the driver flagged us into the side of the road. As the truck rolled to a stop, my heart was thumping and my mouth was dry. I felt certain it was me they were after. My method of escape had been discovered and the troops were on the look-out for me.

Out of the staff car sprang a German major, two German lieutenants and an Italian captain. They came round to the back of the truck and ordered us out. Ettore and Guglielmo were asked for their papers and their destination. One of the lieutenants did all the talking, while the German major stood by. The word '*verboten*' cropped up several times; obviously we had broken some army regulation by accepting a ride in a military vehicle. Then the Italian captain turned to me.

'Where are you going, Father?'

'Pisa,' I told him; and he seemed satisfied. Not so the

German lieutenant, who quickly asked him some question I couldn't understand. He turned back to me.

'Where from?'

'Originally from Monte Cassino,' I said, 'but I've been travelling round the country, visiting the prison camps.'

It was invented, like my Irish nationality had been, on the spur of the moment, but it seemed to convince them, and we were allowed to continue, but on foot.

We all agreed that it had been a close call, but I realized, not for the first time, how perfect my disguise was. My robe and crucifix were a better passport than a membership card of the Nazi party; and although I had already convinced others of my genuineness, this was the first time I'd felt confident enough to address an Italian officer in his own language, and I had passed the test with flying colours. At the same time, I reminded myself not to get too cocky. All I could safely say was that I had got away with it so far, and each successful encounter increased my self-assurance. I knew that Ettore, Guglielmo and I would soon have to part, but now I wasn't really worried. I should certainly miss their company and guidance, but I was beginning to feel I could make it on my own.

We slogged on along the road, feeling very smug at having outsmarted the Germans.

Chapter Eight

WE reached Pisa without further incident, and sat down at an outdoor cafe for a glass of wine. The German and Italian soldiers who occupied several of the tables took no notice of us; but a party of student monks close by were obviously curious; and when we got up to leave, they came over.

'Where are you bound for?' I was asked.

'Grosseto,' I said; it was the first name that came into my mind; and to fend off any more awkward questions I asked them who they were and where they were from. It seemed that they were French novices and had been studying in Rome and Pisa for the past two years. Our conversation was in French, which evidently pleased them, and I introduced them to Ettore and Guglielmo.

I think they would have kept us there all day if we'd let them; but I saw all sorts of pitfalls ahead, since monks, I was sure, talked shop among themselves like any other group of people, and I should have quickly been out of my depth. So we excused ourselves rather hurriedly and, since there was still plenty of daylight left, went on a sight-seeing tour of the city.

We had a look at the cathedral and the leaning tower, and a good many other historic buildings. Ettore and Guglielmo, who had never been there before and probably never would have gone if it hadn't been for me, were just like a couple of tourists, oohing and aahing at the marvels before them. Personally, I would have been much happier to be on our way; but it was nearly dark before I succeeded in getting them back on the road.

That night, staying in a house in Calci, a village east of Pisa, Ettore and Guglielmo told me that they would have to leave me the next day and try to find work. The news shook me, though I tried not to show it. For weeks now, I had had Italians to guide, protect and instruct me; first Guglielmo alone, then him and his uncle; now, at last, I should really be on my own, for the first time since escaping. When we said good night, I went to my room expecting to lie awake worrying; but instead I found myself thinking of Assunta and those four German soldiers who were staying in her house. But even that disturbing thought wasn't enough to keep me awake for long.

*

We were all up early the following morning, and the woman of the house gave us coffee and bread. We didn't speak much; we knew this was to be our last day together, and it caused a certain constraint between us. When Ettore tried to pay for the night's lodging, the woman at first refused; it wasn't every day they had a monk in their house, she said. I had never dreamed that it was possible to travel around a country free, and yet here I was, doing just that. When Ettore pointed out that neither he nor Guglielmo were in Holy Orders, she did accept something – only to insist on providing us with food and wine for the journey.

After a few miles we came to the river Arno, and I told the others I'd like to bathe. We stripped off and dived in. It felt great. I washed out my clothes and let them dry in the sun. A few people passed while we were in the water, but they ignored us. Afterwards, we sat on the bank and went over the route I was to take after we'd parted. I memorized it, and we finished our meal in silence.

That evening, about an hour after sunset, we came to a

61

farm at a place called Stagno, which seemed suitable for our night's lodging, and Ettore made me do the asking; good practice, he said. An old man answered the door, and when I had put the usual question, I introduced the others, and he asked us in. The rest of the family were at dinner; we always picked the right time to barge in on people! We exchanged courtesies, and were told we could sleep in the loft over the barn. Back to the animals, I thought; but it was better than nothing.

We were invited to join them at table, and I had to face the usual battery of questions. They were simple people, and so honoured to have a man of God in their house that they all but ignored Ettore and Guglielmo. Then the talk turned to the war and its problems, and Guglielmo said that he and Ettore were experienced farm labourers and were looking for work. The old man looked hard at them; he needed help, he said, but he couldn't afford to pay very much; the best he could offer them was bed and board and a few lire a week.

It was settled, and they shook hands on it; and I felt my heart sink. How much easier to stop and see the war out in some remote farmstead than press on alone into the unknown. The failure of nerve was only momentary; and here I didn't even have Assunta to make the decision harder.

Later that night, in the loft, we talked for a long time about the past and the future, my future. Ettore gave me all the money he had left, and although I tried to refuse it, I should have known better; he never took no for an answer. I swore that I would see them again some day in better times; and they made me promise that if things got too rough, I would try to make my way back to the Bossi farm. We made all the usual promises friends make at partings; and in that moment of silence which always comes in conversations of this sort, we fell asleep.

The old man woke us in the morning and told us to come

into the house and eat. If anyone had told me, before the war, that one day I would have salami and cheese for breakfast – and enjoy it, I should have laughed. The meal over, I offered to buy some food from the old man to take with me, but he wouldn't hear of it; his wife had already packed some for me; all they asked in return was my blessing. I gave it sincerely and even if I had no right, God would be my judge.

Ettore drew me aside and warned me not to confide in anyone unless I was absolutely sure of them; I hardly needed to be told, but his concern was genuine and I appreciated it. Then the old man reappeared with a pair of trousers, which he pressed on me.

'They don't fit me any more,' he said, 'and you might find them useful when the weather gets cold. Take them!' Truly, these people would give one the clothes off their backs.

The time had come for me to leave. Ettore, Guglielmo and I embraced, and I set off alone on the long road to the south.

Chapter Nine

I HAD been going for an hour or so when a truck stopped, and the driver leaned out and asked me where I was going. To save any complicated explanations, I said 'Roma'.

'Jump in, Padre. I'm going to Civitavecchia. It's on your way.'

I hesitated for a second. Civitavecchia, I knew, was on the coast, 25 miles or so north of Rome, and so well off the route which Ettore had worked out for me; yet it might look suspicious if I refused. So I said *'Grazie'*, and climbed into the cab beside him.

He was a man in his early forties, and as we clattered along he told me about himself. His name was Alfredo, and he'd been in the Abyssinian campaign, just as Ettore had. He had two sons, one of seventeen, and two daughters.

'A pity they're not all girls,' he said.

'Why do you say that?'

'My elder boy's already been called up for the army; he'll be leaving in a few days.' He shrugged. *'Non fa niente.* It'll all be over in six months.'

I longed to ask him why he was so sure, but I was afraid of appearing too curious. I'd had little enough news of the war since my escape, and hadn't liked to buy a newspaper in case it was out of character. I was constantly coming up against my own ignorance of how a monk was supposed to behave, and often, I'm sure, I was more cautious than I need have been.

From the road I could see the sea, and a couple of islands which Alfredo told me were Montecristo and Elba. There were ships lying off the coast, destroyers and transports, probably troop ships. After a time we caught up with a slow-moving convoy of trucks. A soldier in a jeep waved Alfredo to overtake.

'They'll be heading for Civitavecchia,' Alfredo said. 'It's one of the embarkation ports for North Africa.'

It was then that I should have realized the trap I was letting myself be drawn into; but it was so easy, sitting there chatting to Alfredo and counting the miles as they slipped away behind me.

I must have dozed off, for I was jolted awake by the truck stopping. I thought we must be at Civitavecchia, but then I looked out and saw we were at a military checkpoint. I was petrified; but Alfredo didn't seem to be worried, so I quickly consoled myself that it must be a routine occurrence. Alfredo got out of the truck and showed his papers to the guard; after examining them, he turned to me.

'You next.'

There was nothing to do but obey, and I scrambled out of the cab.

'Where are you going?' I thought quickly. There was a church in the distance; I pointed to it and said:

'I'm going there to see Father Ettore; from there I go on to Rome.'

The guard nodded. I was about to get back into the truck when he told me to follow him into the guard shack. I was really scared by this time; in the past, whenever I had been stopped, I had always been allowed to go on after giving my destination.

Inside were two Germans and another Italian. I tried to act nonchalantly, and hoped desperately that I was succeeding. I was given a chair, while the soldiers talked among themselves. Was it me they were discussing? They were speaking

German and all I could catch was an occasional *jawohl* or *sehr gut*. At last they gave Alfredo a piece of paper and directions telling him where to take his load, while I sat there kicking myself for having been such an idiot as to accept the lift. Alfredo departed, and one of the Germans addressed himself to me.

'*Nicht verstehen Deutsch*,' I said; so he changed to Italian, which was even worse than mine. I gathered that I was going to have to wait for the driver to return. This was a relief, since it suggested that they harboured no particular suspicions about me; but it was going to be an uncomfortable period, all the same. I made up my mind that if I got out of that damn guard shack, I would go to the church, as I had said, and ask for shelter for a few days. If . . .

As I sat there, to all outward appearances lost in deep and tranquil meditation, my brain was working like a triphammer, and time seemed to have come to a standstill. The guards, busy about their duties, left me undisturbed; so in the two hours Alfredo was gone, I had plenty of time to suffer arrest, interrogation, torture, and a slow and agonizing death at the hands of the Gestapo. When he finally returned, I was a nervous wreck; and although he was now going through Rome and could drop me off, I'd had enough for one day and asked him to put me down at the church. I needed a little peace and seclusion to recover.

*

A priest came out of the church and stood watching on the steps as I said goodbye to Alfredo. The truck pulled away.

'*Buona sera, Padre*,' I said, 'I am looking for Father Ettore.'

He looked at me quizzically for a moment. 'I know of no such priest in this region.'

I was dumbfounded at the news. 'But I met him in Pisa, and I am sure he said that he lived in this village.'

'I assure you he does not,' he said. 'If he did, I think I

66

should know of it.' His eyes twinkled as he spoke, and I felt encouraged to persevere.

'I must have got it wrong. But could I possibly stay a day or two to rest after my long trip?'

'Of course. Please stay as long as you like.'

Father Anselmo, as he was called, led me to his modest quarters at the rear of the church. He introduced me to Angelina, who was his general help, and showed me to a room which was kept ready for the occasional traveller. It was small, but very neat and clean. He told me to freshen up, and then we would eat.

I returned to the main room which served as kitchen, dining-room and living-room to find the big table spread as if for a banquet. I had been living for so long on cheese, bread and salami that a proper meal with vegetables was a real pleasure, and it was difficult not to make a pig of myself. Over coffee Father Anselmo asked me if I knew any of the priests in the places I had passed through, and mentioned a few names. I said that I knew one or two of them, but not well. To keep the conversation going, I produced one or two names of my own, Father Anthony, for example, and Father Criccitelli. I didn't feel it necessary to explain that both these reverend gentlemen happened to be priests in my own parish of Clerkenwell; nor was I surprised when he had to admit that they were not known to him.

I went to bed and fell asleep right away, to be woken at 5.30 by Father Anselmo in time for Mass at six, for I had somewhat rashly offered to help him serve. I had served Mass when I was a boy, and wished now that I had paid more attention; I felt as if I were fumbling through the whole thing; but nobody noticed. We had eaten nothing, of course, and about 9 o'clock I sneaked up to my room and nibbled some of the salami and bread I had left over. I felt bad about this later, because I discovered Father Anselmo was expecting me to take Holy Communion, which I did. A

67

slip like this made me aware once again how vulnerable I was if I got loose among 'professionals' of the Church; the safest course, I decided, was to tell Father Anselmo the truth. He'd have found out soon enough, and I didn't relish the prospect of having to go on lying to him.

So, after breakfast, I went out of my way to ask him his views on the war. As I had guessed, they were those of any priest in his situation, a fatalistic assumption that God knew what he was about. The conversation shifted to a more personal level, and this gave me the opening I'd been hoping for.

'And where do you come from, Fra Giuseppe?' he asked me.

'I'm English,' I said as casually as I could. He showed no surprise.

'I knew you weren't Italian from your accent. How long have you been studying for the priesthood?'

I had steeled myself to reveal my true nationality; now, if I was serious, I had to put myself totally at his mercy. I swallowed and blurted out:

'I'm not a monk at all. I'm a British prisoner-of-war on the run.'

To his eternal credit, he accepted it calmly.

'You have chosen a hard road, my son. How long do you expect to avoid capture?'

'With the help of people like you . . . I'll manage.'

For a second or two he didn't reply. Then he gave a little shrug.

'You are safe with me. In a war like this, what side can a priest be on except humanity's?' He smiled.

'It's lucky you told me, though. I was going to ask you to help me when I go round the army camps giving Mass and Confession. That wouldn't have done at all!'

We laughed together at this; and I felt a great surge of relief flood through me, just as it had when I confided in Ettore. To deceive a stranger was one thing; the moment that stranger became a friend, the deceit stuck in my throat and choked me.

'You'd better stay here for a bit and polish up your Italian,' Father Anselmo said; and then he went on to tell me that he occasionally had visits from Italian and German officers, in which case I had better stay in the background and let him do the talking.

'If they find out about you,' he said, 'we'll both be in trouble.'

Chapter Ten

In the event, I stayed with Father Anselmo for two weeks. I thrived on Angelina's cooking, and put on weight. This was my fourth month of freedom; my arm had completely healed, and I was in top shape. There was plenty of work to be done in the village, mending fences, ploughing, milking and general farm work. At first, the cows didn't respond too well to my Italian. Who could blame them? I once called one a 'silly cow' and received a very indignant stare. I learnt a lesson from this, though. I was still liable to express exasperation in my own tongue, and this might have taken some explaining if anyone other than the cows had heard me.

Meanwhile, Father Anselmo planned my next move. He set about contacting a friend of his in Frascati, which was 20 kilometres the other side of Rome, on the main route to the south. He proposed telling him the truth, and asking him to pay me for the work I was doing. When I protested, he explained that if I wanted to travel by bus or train, I should have to pay, and therefore I would need money. Only in Rome could a priest travel for nothing. So it was agreed; and while we waited to hear from Frascati, I made myself useful about the place.

I soon became bold enough to make short trips into the village, where I was known as Fra Giuseppe; and as I went quite often, my presence was taken for granted. I was once asked by an Italian soldier to bless a medallion he wore around his neck, and was happy to oblige (I hope it brought him luck); but I was never approached by the Germans. On another occasion, visiting a young woman and her new baby with Anselmo, he suggested that I baptize the child. When I queried the propriety of this, he said gently: 'I'll be right behind you.'

It was after one of these expeditions that I returned to find Father Anselmo thoroughly disturbed. He had had a visit from some German soldiers who were looking for a PoW who had escaped from a camp at Caserta, and was believed to be in the neighbourhood. Although the fact that he had been at Caserta let me out, it meant that the authorities would be on the rampage. I should have to watch my step; but what about him? Was there anything I could do to help him stay free? If I could find him before the military caught up with him, there was a chance.

I told Father Anselmo not to worry; if things got too warm, I would move on. But having decided to try and find the escapee, I went on a discreet round, asking people to keep a lookout for him and to let me know if they heard anything. As Fra Giuseppe, my motives were above suspicion, and they all agreed; but their willingness to co-operate surprised me, none the less. They knew the risks well enough; were they, like Father Anselmo, on humanity's side first and patriots only second? Or was it the hated German presence that made them so lukewarm towards the Axis cause? As with all wars, the masses weren't the ones who wanted to fight; and in this case, I suppose, the fact that the request seemed to come from an official of their beloved church probably had something to do with it. It occurred to me, though, that if the Allies had been on Italian soil, I could have started my own resistance movement there and then!

When I told Father Anselmo what I had done, he was anything but pleased. The Gestapo were sure to be in the area, and he thought it extremely rash to risk setting them on my trail as well. However, good soul that he was, he agreed to help if he could.

A few days later, I overheard some Italians soldiers in the village talking about the escaped prisoner. It seemed that some discarded clothing had been found in the woods, and that the Germans were searching the area, using tracker dogs. If there was anything I could do to save this chap, it had to be done fast.

I had become very friendly with one farmer in particular, Angelo Tornelli. He was a communist and therefore had no time for the Church, a difficulty that I had managed to avoid by never ramming it down his throat; but he had an equal detestation of both Hitler and Mussolini, and this made him a valuable potential ally. I went straight to his farm, told him what I'd heard, and asked for his help.

'Leave it to me,' said Angelo. 'I'll ask around – oh yes, I'll be discreet, don't worry! – and if I find him, I'll look after him and let you know.'

Comforted by the feeling that I had done everything possible, I left him and made my way back to the church.

Two days passed without any further news. I was certain that the man must still be at large, partly because Giusto, the local bobby, was a friend of mine and would have told me of any developments; and partly because the first thing the military normally did was to get hold of the parish priest and tell him to warn his parishioners of the penalties attached to hiding or helping the refugee; and neither of these things had happened. So either he was still in hiding somewhere, or he had given them the slip and left the district altogether.

But then I received a message from Angelo to go to his farm immediately. I hurried over, to find the horses already harnessed to the cart, and Angelo himself in a fever to be away.

'Ah, there you are, Padre! Jump in.'

With a flick of the whip, we were off. As we lurched along the lane, I said:

'What's up? Where are we going? Have you found him?'

Angelo grinned conspiratorially. 'He's found. Carlo, a good friend of mine, is taking care of him.'

It was an hour's drive to Vetralla and Carlo met us in his yard. The man, he said, was in the kitchen; but when we went inside, there was no sign of him. Immediately I suffered one of those traumas of suspicion which affect people on the run. Had I fallen into a trap? Were Angelo and Carlo the farmers they professed to be, or agents of the Gestapo in disguise? It was possible; anything was possible. But my fears were unfounded; Carlo was just feeling me out. Even though I was Fra Giuseppe, there was still a war on.

Carlo's wife gave us some vino and we made small talk. When Angelo thought everyone was at ease, he brought up the subject of escape; without a word, Carlo got up and left the room. He returned a few moments later accompanied by a very nervous young man who, from his fair hair and complexion, one would immediately assume to be English. I was introduced to him as Fra Giuseppe and, speaking in English with an ice-cream vendor's accent, I asked him about himself.

His name was Fred Sheppard, he was from Leek in Staffordshire, and he'd been captured in North Africa ten months before and sent to Campo Basso near Caserta. From there he'd managed to escape, without maps or money or more than a smattering of Italian and German, and set off blind. To begin with he'd stolen some clothes from a farm near the camp; and later, with some idea of altering his disguise, I suppose, he'd stolen some more, leaving the others in the woods. I told him that the Germans had found them, and that he was the object of a most intensive man-hunt. He was very sorry for himself, and, I think, was regretting that he had ever escaped. He had no idea where he was or where he was going.

73

I was able to assure him that he was among friends; but I warned him to keep out of sight as much as possible as, quite apart from the search that was going on, the military frequently visited the farms for supplies.

'I will return tomorrow,' I said, 'bringing other clothes for you, and information to help you on your way.'

His relief and gratitude were quite touching; and I left him still firmly believing that he had been befriended by an English-speaking Italian monk. I knew his feelings, for I had had them myself several times in the past months.

Chapter Eleven

WHEN I went to bed that night, I was more relaxed than I had been since I escaped. I realized that what I had been missing was a true companion. Ettore, Guglielmo, Father Anselmo, were all good friends, but inevitably the difference of nationality and background – and above all language – had stood between us. As a result, and without being fully aware of it, I had merely gone along with the various suggestions they had made, and taken few decisions of my own. I had stayed in one place too long; I had eaten adequately, slept well, and never been in danger of capture; yet with all these advantages, after four months I was still barely halfway to my goal. With another Englishman, however, it would be different. We should encourage each other, spur each other on. Right, I thought, no more complacency, no more apathy! Get off your tail, and get this show on the road!

My brain was racing ahead now, making plans, exploring possibilities. I must look again at the route Ettore had planned, from which I had wandered since leaving Pisa, and try to get back on to it. Fred would need papers–but Angelo had already promised to arrange this. The first thing was to tell Sheppard about myself; take him into my confidence, and then suggest we team up with the single intention of reaching Sicily and finally North Africa. He would have little option but to agree, I thought. He hadn't a clue where he was, and if he kept going in the direction he had been, he would have walked smack into the Germans and been recaptured. Far better for us to go on together. But could a monk and a civilian travel together without looking suspicious? Why not? I'd covered a good many miles with Guglielmo and Ettore, and no one had found it odd. It would be no different with Sheppard. With these thoughts in mind, I fell into a deep, untroubled sleep.

At breakfast next morning, after we had served all the Masses, Father Anselmo asked me my plans. I told him and he agreed with them. Sheppard and I would make for Frascati, where Father Anselmo's friend would give us any further help we needed. First I would go to Angelo to see about the papers; then I would go to Carlo's and tell Sheppard what I had organized.

Angelo said the papers would take about a week. Until they were ready, Sheppard would have to remain in hiding. From Angelo's I went on to Carlo's. Sheppard looked better than he had done the previous night; he'd slept well, and seemed more at ease. I was still bubbling with excitement over my inspiration of the previous evening; but now, quite suddenly, coming face to face with him again, I was struck with doubts and suspicions. Why, I didn't know. His Staffordshire accent seemed genuine enough; he looked and sounded and behaved like an Englishman; yet something warned me to be careful. The Nazis, I knew, were adept at using people either born and raised in England or who had spent years there, to infiltrate into our organizations. They used them, too, as *agents provocateurs* to trap those who assisted escaped PoWs. This sudden access of caution was, I suppose, the obverse of my sudden burst of confidence and resolution of the night before. I was a member of the British forces behind the enemy lines. Admittedly I was only there by accident, not as a trained agent; but I had a duty, all the same, and more than simply to save my own skin. Why else had I not simply stayed put at the Bossi's and settled down with Assunta to see the war out?

I didn't think it out so explicitly at the time; merely, obeying some instinct of wariness, put off revealing myself to Sheppard. Instead, keeping up my monkish role and my broken English accent, I told him that I would help him to get away and set him on the road for the south of Italy. In a few days he would have the necessary papers and new clothes, and then he could get going. In the meantime, he was to lie low. I didn't tell him how far I intended to accompany him, nor our destination and route.

Sheppard himself was overwhelmed by the change in his fortunes.

'What a bit of luck, meeting you, Brother Giuseppe!' he said. 'It's incredible!'

Five days later Fred's papers were ready. Who had forged them I did not know, and didn't ask, but they were perfect. Angelo brought them to me at the church, and invited Father Anselmo and myself to his house for dinner. There was nothing to stop us now from setting off, and the meal would have been a melancholy occasion had it not been for Angelo's robust and caustic humour. I reflected that, though Sheppard thought himself lucky, I was no less lucky myself in having found these two – the mild and truly Christian priest, and the forthright communist farmer – to help me on my way.

That night Father Anselmo gave me a pouch of money subscribed, he said, by his parishioners in gratitude for my help in the village, and his blessing; and before sunrise the following morning I left the priest's house for the last time and made my way to Carlo's. Sheppard, dressed in his new clothes which had been taken there the previous day, was waiting for me. I gave him the papers; we all embraced warmly; and then Sheppard and I set off. Angelo had come over to say goodbye, and I could see that he would have loved to be going with us.

The morning was cool, and although it was still early, it seemed the whole countryside was up to wave us on our way.

As we walked, I studied Sheppard closely. If he was not 'Fred Sheppard', but had been planted by the Gestapo, how could I find out? I sized him up, and thought, 'If he's a plant, I can make short work of him.' There was always the knife Ferruccio Bossi had given me while I was at his farm; I'd kept it, feeling it might come in handy some time, and I knew I wouldn't hesitate to use it. I had come too far and had involved too many people to slip up now. I couldn't decide, and in any case, there was no hurry. In the meantime, we could just keep on walking, and I would keep my eyes and ears open.

Around midday we stopped for a rest and something to eat. It was a good chance to ask him about his background – which was nothing extraordinary: working class family, normal home life. Nothing rang false. When he asked me about myself I made up a story as I went along. He didn't know it, but we were fencing with each other, and all the time I was probing his defences, while keeping my own guard up. Poor, simple Fred Sheppard, suspected of being an agent of the Gestapo! He was wondering if the Red Cross would know of his escape, and, if they did, whether they would notify his family. His father worked in a textile mill, and he had a younger brother in the navy and a sister of fifteen in a munitions factory. His mother would worry if she didn't receive any news of him; I wanted to tell him that I was in the same boat. It was all so naïve and open, I was becoming more and more convinced he was genuine, but I still didn't feel able to trust him.

As we continued on our journey, the road suddenly opened out into a town called Bracciano. It was market day, and it was thronged. I warned Sheppard that there might be German or Italian troops there, and to be on his guard. We headed for the nearest cantina, took a table, and ordered vino. I made him speak Italian to me, which was hilarious. He knew very little anyway, and what he did know was delivered in such a broad northern accent that I burst out laughing. This hurt his feelings; but then he saw the funny side of it, and asked if it might not be better if he pretended to be dumb. Anything rather than his 'Stafford Italian'; and for good measure I suggested that he'd better pretend to be deaf as well. The monk and the deaf-mute; it had a sort of lunatic logic about it, like the blind leading the blind.

Towards evening we came to a small village and asked for a room at the local inn. I was accepted without question, but Shep had to show his papers. It gave him a chance to play his deaf and dumb role, which he carried off convincingly. After dinner we walked round the village and happened to meet the priest, Father Pietro, who stopped to talk to us. When I mentioned Father Anselmo, whom he knew, and told him where we were staying, he insisted that we should move into his house the next day.

'You will be more than welcome,' he said.

That night I briefed Shep on how to conduct himself while we stayed with Father Pietro, including the order of Mass, which we would be expected to attend. When, next morning, we moved into the priest's house and went to church, I was glad to see that he was able to follow the service without any difficulty.

Father Pietro put us on to a local farmer named Bossco, who, he said, would be glad of any help we could give. We went there right away and were both accepted without any bother. Bossco showed us the various jobs that needed to be done, and I translated his instructions into a phoney sign language for Shep's benefit. Bossco, like others I had met, was reluctant to let me work for him, but I assured him that it was quite in order, and indeed a pleasure. At that, he relaxed, and everything went well. We managed to keep up our comedy act of monk and mute successfully; and it was I, not Shep, who was to come unstuck.

Contrary to Father Anselmo's advice and my own

preference, I hadn't told Father Pietro our true identity; it was more difficult than I'd anticipated, in cold blood. Anyway, after dinner on our second night, Father Pietro asked me what Order I belonged to. I had vaguely seconded myself to the Franciscans, simply because Fra Domenico was one; but I knew next to nothing about them, and when faced with Father Pietro's probing questions, I was stumped. I knew I couldn't fool him, so I told him the truth. I mentioned that Father Anselmo had also known, and had helped me; and like that good priest, he took the news very well, and with only mild surprise.

His main concern was that I shouldn't give myself away so carelessly again; his questions about my Order had been no more than polite curiosity, but I'd had no answers ready. I kicked myself for not having 'studied my part' more thoroughly; though in this case it luckily didn't matter, on another occasion it might make the difference between life and death. But one thing was clear; I had no option now but to let Shep in on the secret as well, and the sooner the better.

The opportunity came that night, and I must confess it was worth it, just to see his face. He was absolutely dumbfounded. Once it had finally sunk in, he burst out laughing, and kept slapping me on the back, saying:

'Well I never! You crafty old bugger! I'll be damned! And to think I never twigged. You're a crafty bugger and no mistake!'

After that, we went on talking for hours. He kept on coming back to my method of escape, which was quite new to him; and every now and then he would start chortling again at the thought of how I had fooled everyone, and not least him. I told him about Assunta, and he was green with envy.

'I said you were a crafty bugger,' he repeated, 'and by God you are. What I wouldn't give for a girl right now!'

He didn't once mention his own escape, and for some reason I can't explain, I never asked him! My way of getting out of Campo 303 had been good, certainly; but Shep had also escaped from a well-guarded prison camp yet he didn't think anything of it. I judged him to be a good-hearted bloke but a bit scatter-brained; he would need watching on our journey, particularly if a pretty signorina – he would keep calling them 'fräuleins'! – gave him the eye. I reminded him that we had nothing to prove we were members of the Allied forces, and that if we were caught, we would almost certainly be shot as spies.

Yet, that night, it was difficult to take such perils seriously. Here we were, Paolo Bianchi from Leek, and Fra Giuseppe from Clerkenwell, one posing as a monk and the other as a deaf-mute, in the middle of enemy territory, and without a care in the world. The humour of the situation hit me and I burst into helpless laughter. Shep didn't know what had struck me as so funny, but after a moment or two he caught the infection and started laughing too.

*

Next day we set out for Frascati with Father Pietro's blessing on our heads, and our haversacks loaded with a parting present of food from the Bossco's. Shep's remark to me as we waved goodbye was that he would rather have had their daughter, Yolanda – an idea, I told him, both ungrateful and immoral, though secretly I agreed with him. She was a peach.

Chapter Twelve

IT took us two days to reach Frascati. It was a beautiful town then; later, in the big Allied push through Italy after their invasion, it suffered fearful devastation, I believe. I'm glad we saw it as it was.

Shep and I stopped at a cantina for a glass of wine and a bite to eat. A policeman drifted over to our table and asked us where we were from and where we were going.

'We're on our way from Grosseto to Anzio,' I said.

Shep remained silent; he had a daft sort of expression on his face, and the *poliziotto* glanced at him curiously. I tapped my temple.

'*Egli non e normale*,' I said.

'*Che peccato!*' He shrugged and left us. I realized with relief that it was common curiosity, not official suspicion, that had brought him over.

'What did you say to him?' Shep whispered.

'That you've a screw loose,' I said. Shep laughed.

'The things I do for England!'

From the cantina we could see a level crossing. Two goods trains went through, heading south, loaded with tanks and artillery and heavily guarded – exclusively, I noticed, by Germans. Shep and I looked at each other, and we each knew what the other was thinking. When we'd finished our drinks, we strolled over to the crossing. The gates were worked by a man and wife. We got into conversation with them, and it didn't take long to find out that this was the main route used by the Germans to send material to Naples.

We took our leave of them, and set off once more. Any idea of looking for Father Anselmo's friend had been overlaid by the excitement of this discovery. We decided to stay close to the tracks and try and find out if the trains ran on a regular schedule.

'Wouldn't it be good if we could blow the whole bloody lot up!' Shep said.

'That would hardly be becoming for a monk!' I replied, and Shep laughed; but once the idea had germinated in our minds, we were halfway to trying to think of a serviceable plan. The couple at the crossing had told us of a farmer, Attilio Meglia, who would give us room and board if Shep would help on the farm, so we went to see him, and he agreed to take us in. He didn't want me to work as well, but I insisted. There was plenty to do; but during meals in the farm kitchen and at breaks from work in the fields, we soon gauged the mood of these independent, hard-working people.

For a start, they were fiercely anti-government. The authorities took most of what they grew, and they were constantly trying to devise ways of cheating on the levy. We ourselves saw many searches by soldiers looking for hidden stores of food, and all of them were unsuccessful. This kind of bloodymindedness, which was common throughout the country but especially strong here, was a great reassurance. These farmers were not the stuff of which informers and collaborators are made.

The work was hard, but there were diversions. A lot of the hands on the farm were women, and Shep made a dead set for one of them. He got away with murder because they all thought he was soft in the head; but he wasn't as daft as they thought. He finally succeeded in dating the girl of his choice. He came back very late, and full of the joys of spring. What was worse, he insisted on giving me a blow-by-blow description of the subsequent seduction, which had taken place, I gathered, behind the cow-shed.

'As long as you're in your dressing-gown,' he said – meaning my robes, 'I've got no competition.'

'I'll give you competition,' I said, and meant it.

'Anyway,' I said, 'you can't even speak the lingo.'

Shep grinned. 'You don't need much. She knew what I wanted, and she wanted it too. *Troppo facile!*'

Whereupon he fell fast asleep and snored like a hog all night.

It was more than flesh and blood could stand, and eventually I asked him to fix me up with one of the girl's friends.

'That's a bit risky, isn't it?' he said. 'For a man of the cloth, I mean.'

I gritted my teeth. 'Just introduce us,' I said. 'I'll take care of the risk.'

'And to think,' Shep said, 'I once asked you how monks got on without women, and you gave me all that guff about "thinking of higher things"!'

I was just going to throw something hard and heavy at him when he added: 'What would Assunta say?' and dodged out of the room.

Later that day, he introduced me to Berta and Giuseppina. Giuseppina was his; Berta was allocated to me. I examined her circumspectly. Not bad, I thought; a little plump – but monks, like beggars, can't be choosers. We talked as we worked. I told the girl that I was studying hard, but, what with the war, it was quite difficult to take my vocation seriously. She nodded, suitably impressed – I hoped – by the problems of a priest in the process of losing his principles. Her boy-friend, she said, was in the army in North Africa.

'He'll be suffering, too,' I said; and thought 'that's far enough away'.

'You're not at all like the usual monk,' Berta said, and I could hear Assunta's voice saying the same thing. To be

84

honest, I didn't feel at all like any kind of monk. I couldn't date her, all the same; but that evening, when Shep suggested to the girls that we went for a walk together, it was quite natural that I should be included, to accompany Berta. It also seemed quite natural that we should choose a route that took us by the railway line, which ran close to the farm.

We had both been trying to think of the best way of interfering with it. To blow up a section, we should need explosives, to which we had no access, so we turned our attention to the possibility of jamming the points. The first priority was to survey the track, and the girls would provide us with convincing cover if anyone saw us.

To begin with we didn't learn very much. The Rome-Naples express went through, and several small freight trains, neither of which interested us; but it seemed that the Germans did not keep to a regular schedule, so when the time came we would have to take pot luck. At least we knew there would be a train of theirs some time.

Every evening for a week we went the same way to see if we could figure out a sequence in the German movements. We met nobody, and no one seemed to take the least interest in us; then, on the seventh evening, when it was getting dark, we came face to face with two Italian guards. We probably scared them nearly as badly as they scared us.

'What are you doing here?'

'Just walking.'

'Don't you know it's a forbidden area?'

One of them shone his torch on the girls.

'You're from the Meglia farm, aren't you?'

They admitted they were.

'You should know better. Your papers!' The guards studied Shep's and the girls' papers thoroughly in the light of their torches, but didn't ask for mine, which was fortunate. After a long time they handed them back, and accompanied us to the farm road. There they told us to get going and not to come that way again.

'You were lucky,' said the senior of the two, 'our orders are to shoot on sight. It was only because I saw the padre's robes in the moonlight that we held our fire.'

The girls were crying, and thoroughly frightened, and we wasted no time getting back to the farm. We had indeed been lucky, and I cursed myself for being so careless. It was obvious that a main line, carrying military equipment, would be heavily patrolled, and it was only amazing that we hadn't run into them before. Perhaps there was a security build-up in progress; it seemed reasonable, in which case it suggested that there was a big movement of troops and stores in the offing. Later the girls confirmed that this had happened before; so it looked as if we might have been lucky in more ways than one.

Chapter Thirteen

For a time we kept well away from the tracks. We worked in the fields by day, and stayed around the farm or went into Frascati in the evenings. Our association with Berta and Giuseppina was accepted by the others on the farm, and was satisfactory to all parties. Berta didn't affect me as Assunta had done. She was of coarser grain, extremely passionate, and very possessive – a characteristic I saw might be embarrassing one day. Giuseppina, on the other hand, was quiet and undemonstrative. I knew she liked Shep a lot, but she went out of her way not to show it.

Sunday in Italy is a true day of rest; everything stops; nobody lifts a finger. We used to take advantage of this inactivity to go for long walks with the girls. We didn't go on to the railway track, but we were never far away from it, and it gave us an opportunity to study the lie of the land. It was on one of these walks that we noticed that certain remote lengths of the track were unguarded. We surveyed these sections carefully from a hill, and, to our delight, saw that one of them had a set of points. We selected a place from which we could get a good view of it, and sat down, under the pretext of cuddling with the girls. With an arm round Berta, and my eyes on the railway, I did some rapid thinking.

We should need a good solid iron bar to jam the points. This shouldn't be hard to get; there must be something suitable at the farm. Shep and I always spoke English in front of the girls. I'd told Giuseppina that he was Swiss, and they thought we were talking schweizer-deutsch to each other! So we could discuss our plans quite openly in front of them, and Shep agreed that my idea seemed feasible. No doubt the girls thought that our excitement was all on their account!

*

Suddenly everything was falling into place. It was time to be moving on, and this should be our farewell gesture to Frascati. Shep agreed. He had had enough of Giuseppina and wanted to get away too. We let it be known, gently, that we were leaving. As I anticipated, Berta wanted to come with us, and I had to be very firm with her. I was going to continue my studies, I said sternly, and from now on there would be no room for women in my life. She cried piteously, but this was very different from parting with Assunta. This time I had a clear objective – I was determined to do some damage to a German train, and then carry on with our journey south. Shep had a little bother too, but Giuseppina was easier to pacify.

He'd found just the thing to jam the points, a steel rod, about four feet long, which had been part of a piece of farm equipment. He stowed this in a safe place, ready for our departure. I was very glad of his company now; I was sure I couldn't have mounted this operation alone. My main anxiety was that, if we succeeded at all, we should merely derail some ordinary passenger train, for we had been unable to glean any information on the movement of military traffic. We had tried quizzing Santo, the crossing keeper, but all I could gather from him was that the Germans moved equipment as it became available to them in the north, and that traffic was increasing on the line as they tried to transfer as much as possible southward before winter finally set in.

Santo had an idea that something was on, though; he'd heard a rumour that the Germans were about to invade Malta. This news was bad, if it was true, for if the Germans

88

occupied Malta they would command the Mediterranean, and the Allied cause there would be as good as lost. We did find out one important thing; the trains always came through in groups of three, two carrying troops and one long freight train, usually loaded with tanks and other heavy equipment, and usually at night.

I told Santo that we wanted to get to Cassino, and asked him if he thought it might be possible for us to get a ride on a troop train. He shook his head vehemently.

'Not a chance! But why not take the passenger train? It runs twice a week, and stops here if there are any passengers. It goes through to Cassino.'

I thanked him warmly. I'd found out what I wanted to know: the day and the time the civilian trains passed. With this information, it was at least possible to work out when *not* to sabotage the line. The rest had to depend on luck.

The last evening at the farm we met the girls as usual, and took them for a walk once more to the hill that overlooked the railway. I had hidden the steel bar in my robes; and when we sat down I pulled it out, taking care to hide it from Berta, and threw it behind me into some bushes. It wouldn't be hard to find when we needed it. Berta grabbed me and, smothering me with kisses, begged me not to leave.

'I'm sorry,' I said, 'I have to. I can't change my plans now.'

She began to sulk, so I just lay on my back, waiting for her next move; this, I knew, would be to snuggle close to me. Which, quite soon, she did.

'You don't really want to leave me, Giuseppe, do you?'

'Of course I don't *want* to, *prediletto*,' I said. 'But I have made my vows.' (God forgive me.) 'I can't go back on them.'

As I thought about it, I was glad I hadn't confided in Berta. If she'd known who I really was, I'm sure she would have blackmailed me into staying.

89

We took the girls back, and Shep and I went to our room. Next morning we said our goodbyes at the farm, and took the road which ran parallel with the railway. After about a mile, we left it and made our way to the hill above the points. I found the steel bar. Now there was nothing to do but wait for the night.

Once the sun had set, the dark came quickly. We slipped carefully and quietly down to the tracks, and found the points. We had never seen guards on this section, and there was no sign of any now. Quickly we set to work. One end of the bar was flattened, almost like a crowbar, and this we jammed between the rails as a lever. Together we flung our weight on it; the rail began to move. We heaved harder, and managed to prise them about six inches apart. That should do. We left the bar in the gap, wedged in the V we had made by levering the rails apart. If the train was travelling fast, it should jump the track with spectacular results; if it was travelling slowly, it would certainly be derailed, and cause obstruction and delay. All we needed was the right train.

As soon as we had done the work, we set off back to the road and headed south. We hadn't been walking for more than ten minutes when we heard a train whistle. It came from behind us, so it must have been whistling for the level crossing at Frascati. We stopped, holding our breath, listening in the quietness of the night, wondering what we were going to hear.

The roar of the train grew louder, the rhythmic thunder of the wheels increased, then changed abruptly to a screeching and squealing that set my teeth on edge. For a split second there was silence. Then the night was torn apart by a terrific explosion, and another, and another. A great flash lit up the sky all round, the sparks falling like Greek fire into the darkling woods. It sounded as if we had got an ammunition train. We stood for a moment; we were trembling with excitement and tension. This was more dramatic than we had ever dreamed.

'Jesus!' Shep whispered. 'Did we do that?'

'I think so,' I said. 'Let's get the hell out!'

Chapter Fourteen

WE skirted Palestrina in the darkness, and at first light came to a farm. There was a light in one of the downstairs windows, and as we walked into the yard an enormous dog started barking and snarling, hurling itself in our direction to the full length of its chain. We edged our way round this monster, praying that the chain would hold, and knocked at the door. It was opened by a young woman.

'*Buon giorno, signorina,*' I said in my most unctuous manner, 'do you know where we might find food and shelter for a few days in return for work?'

She didn't answer, but called 'Padre!' over her shoulder. An older man came to the door. He looked at us closely, then, reassured presumably by my robes, asked us in and introduced himself, over coffee and food, as Biaggio Longo.

'You can stay here,' he said. 'My son's away in the navy. You're welcome to use his room.'

'*Grazie.*'

We were bone-tired after the night's adventures, and as soon as we had finished our coffee, his daughter showed us the room and we went to bed.

We had only been asleep for a few minutes when Biaggio woke us urgently. The *carabiniere* were downstairs and were asking about us. Shep, startled at being woken so suddenly, came out with a few choice words in English. I nearly had a fit. Biaggio, I thought, looked at him curiously, and I quickly covered up.

'He's Swiss,' I said, 'and – ' tapping my forehead, 'not quite all there.' This always needled Shep, but there was nothing he could do about it.

In the kitchen were two *carabiniere*, and – more worrying – one of the Fascist secret police. They questioned me briefly, and then demanded to see Shep's papers. These they examined minutely, and it was obvious that they weren't satisfied. There was a conference between them; at last the secret policeman took Shep roughly by the arm.

'You, come with me.'

Shep shrugged, and I explained that he was a little simple, and that I was taking him to a monastery where he would be looked after. I felt they believed me, but they still insisted that Shep had to go with them. I made as if to go too, but they wouldn't have it.

'I don't expect we shall have to keep him long.'

As if solicitous for his welfare – as indeed I was, and my own! – I put my arm round his shoulder and whispered, 'Keep up the idiot act!' Shep gave me his best moron stare, and, when he was sure they weren't looking, the ghost of a wink.

The next few hours seemed like an eternity. If they connected him with the train incident, I knew they would be back for me and we would be sunk. Finally, Shep returned. He had not understood all that had been said; but he'd been taken to the local police station, where there were other Fascist policemen, and some German soldiers as well. He gathered that they were discussing the train crash, and that there had been a lot of damage. He had been questioned, but he'd acted dumb and just kept asking for me. In the end they gave up and let him go. Longo gave him a brandy to cheer him up.

*

I was worried sick, not least because they'd got on to us

93

so quickly; but Longo said it was perfectly normal: they always checked up on strangers. And after what had happened on the railway! He had already heard, via the grapevine, that a train carrying troops and ammunition had come off the rails, and, inevitably, sabotage was suspected. He didn't know the details, but it was being said that it would take several days to clear the track. Very satisfactory. I would have given a lot to see the damage.

Dinner that evening seemed something special, a sort of secret celebration of the job we had done. After I said grace, Shep was in the habit of saying 'Oh Lord, let it not be our last'. Longo and his daughter were convinced he was Swiss and completely mad, so they didn't suspect anything. But that evening the words seemed to hold a particular meaning.

*

It was now November, and the rainy season was setting in. And did it rain! Anyone who has been in Italy at that time of year will know what I mean. It wasn't too cold yet, but the dampness was almost worse. Either way, it was bad for foot travellers, and we wondered whether we should try and settle in somewhere until the rains and the winter were over. It was a depressing thought. I felt utterly cut off from the war, from my family, from life almost. There was no radio at Longo's so we heard no news, only local rumours and gossip.

From this source, we learned that the train wreck had been put down to the driver coming up to the points too fast, causing it to jump the tracks, and that there had been a lot of casualties, both Italian and German. The exploding ammunition had ripped up the track, causing even more delay. That was cheering, but didn't solve our immediate problems.

For the moment, there was nothing to do but stay on at the Longo farm and make the best use of our time we could.

There was not much work to be done because of the weather, so we were very bored and unsettled. The local priest, Don Pesce – Shep referred to him as 'The Fish' – lent me some books, and Shep and I worked on improving our Italian. Learning a language is like learning to swim: if you really have to, you do. And we really had to.

At about this time there was a big build-up of men and material in the area. The soldiers had been issued with tropical kit, so we knew they were going to North Africa. I saw a lot of them at church when they attended Mass, and often had a chance to talk to them afterwards; and Shep and I sometimes came across them in the village cantina. These fortuitous meetings weren't always without incident. On one occasion a drunken German soldier came lurching over to our table. I didn't understand what he said but it was obviously uncomplimentary; he stood in front of us shouting, and then brought his act to a finale by spitting on the floor at my feet. At that point, one of his mates came and took him away. Shep, who knew some German, told me afterwards that he'd been railing at the church and all it stood for. I said, 'Perhaps he was bitten by a nun as a child.'

One drawback from our point of view was that the girls – like girls everywhere – had eyes only for the soldiers. They had a great time, and we were dead out of luck. What could a mere monk or a semi-imbecile do to compete with the brave flower of the Wehrmacht and the *Esercito Italiano*? Mind you, it was probably a good thing we didn't become involved with any girls; we were vulnerable enough without that.

Out of my casual encounters with the troops came a request to teach some of the Germans Italian, in return for German lessons, which I accepted. As a result, after a very short time, I picked up a good smattering of the language. This was only one instance of how we had become an accepted part of the village scene. In the same way, if there was a wedding or an engagement party, we tended to be included.

At one of these, the fiancée, named Lettizia, had been rather sweet on Shep for a time, but neither of them let on! We enjoyed the party, not least the irony of mixing on equal terms with German and Italian soldiers. This was something I could never have visualized in a million years!

Chapter Fifteen

THERE were a lot of communists among the locals; and remembering Angelo Tornelli, I went out of my way to make contact with them. As we both had reason to know, they could be very useful. One in particular who interested me was Aldo Mora. He was very forthright, and indeed seemed to be a sort of spokesman for the others. He was convinced that the Axis would eventually lose the war; England, he said, had the strength of America behind her, and this would make all the difference. I asked him if he wasn't afraid of voicing such inflammatory opinions.

'You're a man of the Church, Fra Giuseppe,' he said, smiling, and put his finger to his lips. 'You'll keep my views to yourself, I'm sure.' He was right. I needed Aldo Mora.

Don Pesce, the priest, he said, knew his attitude well enough.

'All I want is to see this idiotic war ended.' I took due note.

'Just supposing,' I asked him, 'you came across an escaped Allied prisoner-of-war?'

'I would help him, of course.' He went on to tell me that, before the war, he had worked in the West End of London. He had lived in a house in Old Compton Street owned by a Mr Rossi, and had worked at Pinoli's in Wardour Street.

'I like England; people were very good to me while I was there, so . . .' he shrugged expressively, 'I would only be returning a favour.'

He told me a lot more about the time he had spent in London.

'*Parla Inglese?*' I asked him.

'Of course,' he said, 'I was there for three years.' This, I thought, might be a real break.

Aldo took us into Sora and Frosinone, two fairly large towns, where he sold his vegetables and other produce on market days. There were a lot of Germans about but they didn't bother anyone; they were too busy trying to pick up girls. Aldo seemed to be very well known in both towns. Shep helped him with his stall while I wandered around looking the places over. The feeling between the German and Italian soldiers reminded me of that which existed between the Americans and the British. The Germans were better paid and big spenders, and the Italians weren't happy about the competition.

Shep was becoming very brazen now. I watched him discussing the prices of items with German soldiers; he even asked them where they came from and where they were stationed. The majority, it seemed, were at Campo Basso, not far from Sora, which, Aldo told us, was a very large base, accommodating thousands of troops.

We enjoyed our trips with him. In addition, he paid Shep a few lire for helping him on the stall, money which Shep put aside for us to use later. He had grown a large bushy moustache like most of the Italian men, and I had had my beard trimmed and my hair cut very short. I often wondered if I shouldn't have had my head shaved; but I got away with just a crew-cut. I felt sure that I could have gone back to Campo 303 and not been recognized. But I didn't put this to the test!

Autumn was steadily declining into winter. It hadn't snowed yet, but it was getting much colder, and we both thought that we would be staying where we were until the spring. On the whole we were very cheerful; we were accepted by everyone in the neighbourhood, and we spent most evenings with Aldo and his family. He was quite a character, friendly, outspoken, dogmatic in his political views, and very well informed about the war. It was he who told us of the North African landings and Rommel's defeat at El Alamein. The German High Command was diverting supplies from the desert to the Russian front, Aldo said; much good that would do. The Russian front had crumbled because Hitler had underrated the Russian winter, and the resistance put up by the Russian civilians. The Italian army, he said, was dreading being sent to that front to reinforce the dispirited Wehrmacht.

'Hitler was crazy to commit himself to war on two fronts,' Aldo said. 'And what's the result? Rommel, a great general, a great military tactician, is being starved of supplies.'

It looked as if, at last, the war was beginning to go our way. The larger cities in the north of Italy – Turin, in particular – were being bombed regularly, and German industry was taking a pasting.

Aldo also mentioned the train crash we had caused. In his opinion, he said, it was sabotage, and not its speed, that had derailed it. I asked why. He shrugged his shoulders:

'There are many people who would do it in order to harm the Germans or the Fascisti.'

I was becoming concerned about my robes, which were getting very tattered; but Don Pesce arranged for a seamstress in the village to make me some new ones. My sandals were just as bad; they had more holes than a gruyère cheese; but I managed to cadge some boots from a woman whose husband was away in the army. They were on the big side, but I wasn't in a position to complain, especially as footwear was almost unobtainable. Shep had picked up a new suit and some more shoes, so we were both well equipped.

We still went to the markets with Aldo, which helped break the monotony; and there were meetings at his house two or three times a week, which we were allowed to attend. The same men came each time, and although I didn't realize it then, this was a communist cell. The evening usually started with a game of cards and went on to a discussion. Shep and I never became involved, but we listened to everything and drew our own conclusions.

One day Aldo told us that several Allied aircraft had been shot down during raids on Milan and Bologna, but none of the crews had been found, dead or alive. This could only mean that they were on the run. They couldn't have picked a worse time of year for it, nor a worse place, for the north was overrun with Germans. Aldo agreed that their chances of escaping were slim; and we were too far south to be of any help to them, which was a sad thing. Although, with Christmas coming, we sometimes felt homesick, their probable fate underlined our own amazing good fortune.

Chapter Sixteen

CHRISTMAS came; Christmas, 1942. Whoever would have dreamed that I should be spending it in an Italian village, the well-known, popular Fra Giuseppe who helped to serve Mass and laid on a party for the kids. This was something quite novel and the parents were as delighted as the children. Their gratitude and trust gave us a sense of security.

On Christmas Day it snowed all day long, and it was very cold. Coal was expensive and the people burned logs, which were plentiful. Shep and I helped bring in the firewood. At night we heard a lot of howling, which we thought was dogs, but we were told that it was the howling of wolves. When winter came and food was scarce, they crept out of the woods and foraged around the farms, killing chickens and sheep, and even cattle and small children. The farmers never went out without their guns, and we saw a wolf which one of them had got. It was huge, bigger than a full-grown Alsatian dog, and much fiercer-looking.

Another menace was the eagles, which often carried off lambs, and would also attack people if provoked. They were a majestic sight as they circled, searching for their prey; but what with them and the wolves, and the snow, we were glad we hadn't decided to carry on with our trek.

Aldo also kept us up-to-date on the news. The German armies had been routed in Russia, and the Afrika Korps was in full retreat across the desert. England was being ruthlessly bombed, and, in retaliation, the RAF was stepping up its bomber campaign against Germany. The war was still in the balance; but very slowly it seemed to be tilting in our favour as the might of America was deployed in Europe as well as in the Pacific.

So the months of the winter passed pleasantly enough; but as the days began to lengthen and the weather improved, we had to think about moving on. Needless to say, Shep had become involved with a woman again, this time a young widow in the village. Her name was Maria Felice, and she was undoubtedly attractive; I saw trouble ahead when the time came for us to leave, though she might be useful to us in the meantime.

During the winter our ideas of trying some more sabotage had rather gone into cold storage, but with the spring they revived. Our conversations with Aldo, and our interpretation of the mood of his meetings, encouraged us to think we had an ally there. But first we had to tell him the truth about ourselves. I brooded about this for weeks, looking for the right opportunity.

It came, finally, one evening when we were alone with him in his house, and it fairly bowled him over. We went on to tell him that it was us who had wrecked the train at Frascati. I don't think he believed us at first but, when we told him the details he was convinced. His honest eyes went as round as marbles, and he helped himself to a swig of brandy.

'*Meraviglioso!*' he kept muttering, '*Incredibile!*' And he slapped us on the back and poured out more brandy all round. At last he calmed down, and asked soberly:

'So? What next?'

'We want to continue the good work,' I said. 'Last time we succeeded, by pure luck. We can't rely on that again.'

Aldo nodded. 'There's plenty of scope, but . . .'

'How about explosives?'

'I know someone, yes . . . his name's Gino; he used to be a blaster in the marble quarries at Carrara.'

'Can you trust him?'

'Not sure. I'll find out.'

'Any others who might be interested?'

'Of course. All good *communisti*; you can trust them utterly. Leave it to me.'

A week after this, Aldo invited us to a meeting at his house.

'Don't be surprised if you recognize some of the people there.'

But I was, all the same. There, gathered round the table in Aldo's kitchen were the Mayor, the village policeman, Desimono, the owner of the local cafe, several well-respected businessmen, and the priest, Father Pesce. He was the only one there, apart from Aldo, who knew our identity. The others were there because they were dedicated communists, not because of their social position. A gathering such as this was quite illegal – but in that company we were safe enough! Aldo's wife brought us some vino and glasses and left us.

When everyone had settled down, Aldo said he had called the meeting because something very important had come up and he wanted to tell them about it. In the sudden quiet tension, he threw us a questioning glance; I nodded, and he went on, with a dramatic gesture in our direction.

'It concerns these two young men.'

Everyone stared at us, wondering what was coming next. The whole village, he said, had been very grateful for the help we had given them; we had become true members of the community. Everyone nodded their agreement. Aldo paused; he had an actor's sense of timing. Apart from himself, he said, there was only one person in the village who knew our true identity, and this was Father Pesce. Everyone was looking our way now with puzzled expressions on their faces, and muttering, '*Chi sono?*', who are they?

Aldo waited for silence, and then asked Father Pesce to

take over. The priest stood up and introduced me. Fra Giuseppe, he said, was not a monk at all, but an escaped English prisoner-of-war who had been free since the previous July; and Paolo was the very prisoner who had escaped from the camp at Caserta and of whom they had all heard. There was a second or two of shocked silence. Then we were bombarded with questions about the time between our escape and our arrival in the village. Aldo interrupted them to say that, in addition, we had been responsible for the train that had been sabotaged at Frascati, and we were looking for help to carry out further similar operations. Two of the men, Gino Caligari and Giovanni Adeoni, said they could handle the explosives all right, but where were the targets? There was nothing important in this area, apart from the army base at Sora; if we wanted to do the *Tedeschi* a bad turn, we should have to look further afield. How about Benevento? someone suggested, and there was a murmur of agreement. It was situated more or less in the middle of the country about 30 miles from Naples, and about 100 miles from Bari on the Adriatic coast. It was here that the supply trains from the north split up, for these two ports, or for Brindisi, 50 miles further south.

Once Benevento had been agreed as a likely spot for our activities, it was suggested that Aldo, Gino, Giovanni, Shep and myself should follow the markets south until we found a suitable target. Of course, with Rommel already defeated, supplies were no longer needed in the desert, but with the strong possibility of an Allied invasion of Italy, the material would still be needed on the mainland. If we could destroy even a part of it, it would be a help to the invading forces. The other members of the cell would help by getting what information they could about troop movements and so forth.

Everyone was talking at once now, and we found ourselves swept along by the Italians' gift for instant dramatization. By the end of it, we not only felt that we had been accorded the status of heroes, but that, once we had got into our stride, the war would be as good as won! In this mood of elation, the meeting finally broke up.

*

Two days after this, Aldo came and told us to be ready to move at once. We were to travel in his farm-cart, pulled by his horse Clementina, and with a load of produce on board. There was a market in Benevento, so we could set up our stall while we looked around and decided on our next move.

It wasn't the most luxurious mode of travel; and as we went along, the vegetables – which we were sitting on – began to lose some of their freshness. By the time we reached our destination, I couldn't see that Aldo would have anything fit to sell: but he seemed to know what he was doing, so I didn't question him.

We arrived on the afternoon of the fourth day. It was a busy, bustling town, and crammed with troops, among them, I noticed with some alarm, a number of SS. They looked us over with their hard, professional eyes, but that was all. We made our way to the *piazza del mercato*, Aldo set up his stall, and salvaged what was left of the vegetables in the cart and set them out. Giovanni stayed with him, while Gino took Shep and me to the house of a friend of his by the name of Berto Salvo. Berto greeted him like a long-lost son and, after the inevitable *bottiglia*, asked how long we were staying in Benevento and offered us a room. We accepted gladly, and then we went back to the market.

From what we had seen and learnt, there wasn't much scope for us in Benevento; so that evening, after Aldo had closed up his stall and we were having a meal in a cantina, we decided to go on to Bari in the morning. It meant another four days on the cart, and as Aldo's vegetables were rotting it would involve buying some fresh stuff on the way if we were to maintain our cover as farmers on their way to market.

Back at Berto's, we heard that Bari had been bombed frequently in the last few weeks, and the Italians and Germans had been using it intensively. Berto's own son had embarked there on his way to Africa; he hadn't heard from him for weeks, the last letter he'd received had been posted at Derna, now way behind the 8th Army's lines. When we finally went to bed, we left Berto in melancholy mood, morbidly drinking and brooding about his son.

We left Benevento as planned and went jogging along the main road to Bari. We were passed by innumerable troop convoys on the way, but now there were few waves or smiles for the travelling friar. The soldiers all looked very grim – as well they might.

On our third day out we stopped at a large farm, and Aldo stocked up with more produce. As we moved south, so the poverty became more and more evident. The people were not really short of food, but other things seemed unobtainable. They were mostly illiterate, and largely communist; they and Aldo were on the same wavelength.

We arrived at Bari around noon and headed for the market place. Aldo made the necessary arrangements, and set up his stall. Bari, too, was seething with Germans, and I noticed that they all carried their rifles with them, even off-duty. I guessed they were at a point when they didn't know where the next blow would fall, and didn't even trust their own allies very far. I warned Shep to be on his guard, but such warnings were hardly necessary any more. Like myself, he was much more experienced now than when we had first met. That seemed a long time ago.

When Aldo had organized his stall, he and the others went off to the Ministry of the Interior with their papers in order to be issued with identity cards, as Bari was a prohibited area. I waited for them in a church which was just off the market place; when Aldo picked me up there an hour later, I saw at once that something was wrong. Gino had been detained by the Fascist police, because he was of conscription age and they wanted to know more about him. I immediately thought of Shep; why hadn't they detained him also? He had put on his 'simple' act and they had accepted him as exempt from army service. It was proving as serviceable a disguise as my robes and crucifix.

We settled down to wait for Gino; and when he finally showed up, at about ten, we'd almost decided that they had roped him in for good. Apparently the authorities had suspected him of being a deserter, and not just a draft-dodger, and they'd checked him all the way back to Frascati. But they hadn't found anything wrong, so they let him go. He'd been questioned about the rest of us, but this hadn't been pursued very far; the market, it seemed, was a good enough reason for us to be there. Now, perhaps, we could get down to work.

Chapter Seventeen

EARLY the next morning I went to the church and sat through Mass, and then found my way back to the cantina we had been in the previous night. The others were all there, eating breakfast. We talked over the situation; Giovanni thought it would be a good idea if some of us took jobs.

'That way,' he said, 'we can stay here, we'll have passes, and we'll have a better chance of finding what we're looking for.'

This seemed to make sense, so Aldo and Giovanni went off to look for work. We met in the cantina again that same afternoon; they'd been taken on at the docks, to begin the following morning; better still, they'd made arrangements for Gino and Shep to see the manager. I was a little uneasy about Shep going to work, but luck seemed to be with us, so I didn't raise any objection.

Everything worked out even better than we'd planned. Shep and Gino were duly signed on, and found themselves labouring in, of all places, the oil storage area! What a break! There were millions of gallons of fuel oil and petrol stored there, all of inestimable value to the Axis war machine, all highly inflammable!

This, then, was our target. For a week Shep and Giovanni studied the patrols who guarded the depot, and noted their routes and changeover times. They found one or two loopholes, stretches of wire that received only occasional inspection, and they were sure we could get in without being spotted. With this information, we planned the job carefully, and concluded that it could be done in fifteen minutes. Now it was just a matter of choosing the right moment. We decided that the best time would be during an air raid; Bari had been recently bombed, and we knew that it was a target for the RAF and the Americans. There was only one danger, and that was from our own bombs, but this was a risk we should have to face.

We waited patiently each night; there were a few minor raids, but we wanted to wait for a big one, and go in when the anti-aircraft batteries started, and the noise and confusion would cover our activities.

On the sixth night we had been waiting as usual, and around midnight we gave up, went off to our various quarters, and turned in. I hadn't been asleep very long when I was roughly woken up. It was Aldo, whose room was next to mine. Through a fog of sleep I heard the air raid sirens, and then the drone of aircraft. Then the ack-ack opened up. I jerked myself into full consciousness. Was this our chance? I quickly dressed while Aldo went and woke the others.

There was no moon, but the night sky was laced with searchlight beams and vivid with the flash of gunfire. We made our way to the docks, keeping to alleys and side-streets, and crept along the wire until we came to the place where Giovanni had cut it earlier, a ragged gap, low down behind a stack of empty drums. It was quite deserted. One after another we crawled through, Gino and Giovanni with sticks of dynamite which Shep had stolen from the docks, under their coats.

We reached the storage area without seeing any guards. Gino and Giovanni laid their explosives around one of the massive tanks. It was clearly marked 'Benzina' – petrol. I prayed it wasn't empty. Aldo carried the detonator box, and after attaching the fuse, we stole back to the fence. The planes were overhead now, their bombs were falling in the docks and among the ships alongside. As soon as we were through the fence, Aldo pushed the plunger.

There was a fraction of a second's pause, and then an almighty explosion. We had all taken shelter, but it made little difference; we were sent reeling by the sheer violence of the blast. I staggered to my feet, and then I was running for my life. There were more explosions; I could feel the tremendous heat searing my back, and flames and a dense wall of smoke surged through the depot.

As soon as I was clear of the heat and smoke, I waited for the others – Aldo, Giovanni, Shep – but no sign of Gino. We hung about for a while, but there was no question of going back. The depot was an inferno. Elated, yet heavy of heart, we slipped through the back streets to our cantina. The town was in pandemonium, with fire engines roaring by, people running everywhere, and, from the direction of the docks, a bright glow in the sky topped by a pall of thick black smoke. 'They'll never put out those fires,' I thought; and at that moment another wave of bombers came in. They were putting the beacon we had lit to good advantage. From all round the docks came the whine and crump of bombs. Well, we'd given them something to aim at – and no doubt they would be shooting a great line about their 'direct hits on the oil storage tanks' when they landed. Let 'em.

The next morning, while the others went to work as usual, I went to the church and Mass. Afterwards the priest asked me to accompany him to the docks to see if we could be of any help.

The whole area was completely devastated; the oil and petrol tanks were still burning fiercely, and there were charred bodies lying around. I searched for any sign of Gino, without success. In the harbour, virtually every ship had either been sunk or badly damaged, the tracks in the dockside marshalling yard were torn up like so much wire, and the German army barracks nearby had been flattened.

The dead and wounded were still being brought out of the wreckage. We did what we could, but for many of them the only comfort the priest could offer was the Last Rites.

The smell of burnt flesh was so overpowering that I had to turn away at last and vomit. German and Italian troops were loading the bodies on to flat-bed trucks and taking them to a communal burial plot. I worked all that day helping to take the wounded to a temporary hospital which had been set up. When I left, at sunset, the casualties were still being brought in, and the fires were still burning. According to the radio, fourteen planes had been shot down, but the actual number, I heard later, was three. So much for propaganda. Several of the crews had baled out, but there was so much confusion everywhere that I couldn't find out where they had been taken.

That evening, the priest came and told us that Gino's body had been found near the depot. We felt we must go and pay our last respects, though we feared being identified with him, as part of a group. He was hardly recognizable: one side of his face was burnt to a cinder, one foot had been completely severed, and a chunk of shrapnel had pierced his shoulder, coming out through his chest. I wished I hadn't gone. The priest murmured a prayer for his soul, and sorrowfully we left him to the burial teams. He was our only casualty, but his loss was none the less grievous for that.

Chapter Eighteen

WE left for Brindisi the next day. There were a number of reasons for the move. All traffic was being diverted there, and Bari itself was at a standstill. We had done all we could there anyway, and were better out of the area. Brindisi, we thought, should have distinct possibilities.

We made good time and got there after only two days on the road. Aldo and the others went straight to the docks, and, armed with a letter of recommendation from Bari, got jobs. I had a look round the town. It wasn't as big as Bari, but still a considerable port. There were plenty of soldiers about; their morale seemed high enough, and they were in a spending mood. Two whom I talked to said that they were expecting to go to Bari, but their train had been diverted. What had happened? I merely told them that the town had been heavily raided, but didn't go into details.

There were lots of girls around, as there always are where there are soldiers about. Their presence reminded me sharply of Assunta, so on impulse I bought a postcard and sent it to her. I couldn't say much, but she would at least know where I was.

Aldo had had a good look round the docks, which, he said, were crammed with tanks, heavy guns, trucks and ammunition, and with a lot more equipment coming in, owing to the damage to Bari. This sounded interesting, and I decided to try and have a look for myself. What excuse could I find to get near the ships?

Next day, when the others had gone to work, I went to the church and had a word with the priest. Would it be possible for me to get aboard the hospital ship *Talamba*, which was in port? He didn't see why not, if I had a good reason, and suggested that I asked to see the personnel officer. I didn't believe it could be that easy, but it seemed worth a try. At the dock gate the policeman on duty called the *Talamba* on a ship-to-shore phone and told them he had a priest who wished to visit the wounded, had they any objection? Apparently they had none, for my request was approved without more ado.

On my walk through the dockyard I passed three sizeable troopships, the *Conte Biancamino*, the *Conte Rosso*, and the *Giulio Cesare*. They all had troops on board and there was a lot of activity round them.

The sentry at the gangway of the *Talamba* halted me and checked with the bridge; after a brief exchange I was allowed on board, to be met at the head of the gangway by an orderly and a nurse. At my request they took me below decks to the wards, which were full of Italian and German wounded. I spoke to some of them; they were all casualties from Monty's advance in the Western Desert.

One of the sisters invited me to have lunch on board. Afterwards I went ashore, and as I walked back along the docks, I suddenly wondered what would happen if I tried to get aboard any of the other ships. I chose the *Giulio Cesare*, and walked calmly to the foot of the gangway. The sentry let me pass with no more than a glance and a '*Buon giorno, Padre*'. The casualness of it amazed me, particularly as she was a troopship. On deck an officer asked if he could help me. I told him I was looking for a Domenico Salvo who, I understood, was an officer on the *Cesare*. He didn't know anyone by that name – which was hardly surprising – and suggested I tried the purser's office. This was as good as an invitation to wander around as I liked.

Only once after that was I asked my business – when I was having a look at the cargo deck – and when I told the officer who approached me that I had come to visit the men before they sailed, he accepted it without demur. In any case he was probably too busy to bother about me. But from what I'd seen, I concluded that it wouldn't be too difficult for one or two determined men to sabotage her. A few strategically-placed bundles of rags, treated so that they would self-combust, would soon start fires. Moreover, the operation could be set up in port, to take effect after the ship was at sea.

The promenade deck was crammed with men who had already settled in their chosen spots for the trip. I strolled among them – a word here, a blessing there – for all the world like an army chaplain. It was a very strange feeling: a cold, remote observer in my mind watched every action critically, while all the rest was totally absorbed in the masquerade.

After that performance, I was hot and wanted a drink. Why not the wardroom? One of the crew directed me to it, and I went in. I was quickly made welcome. The steward brought me vermouth on ice, and introduced me to the First Officer. Others drifted over, and I found myself describing some of my wanderings. Then one of them asked me about Rome. Had I been to the Vatican? What did I think of St Peter's Square? I felt the warning light flick on in my brain, remembering how Father Anselmo had trapped me. I hadn't been to Rome, but I had slipped up earlier in the conversation by implying that I had.

'It was so long ago,' I said, 'I've really forgotten.' After that I was more careful, diplomatically changing the subject whenever an awkward question came up.

When the time came for me to leave, the First Officer accompanied me to the gangway.

'Come on board whenever you like. You'll be most welcome.'

It was an invitation I should find hard to resist.

Chapter Nineteen

THAT evening we held a council of war. When I told them about my day's exploits, they were all surprised that I had been allowed so much freedom.

'It's gives us an opening that's too good to miss,' I said. Giovanni objected that the whole scheme was far too risky, but I disagreed. Even if we couldn't actually disable a ship, we might at least be able to delay her departure, and we should have gained something.

We tossed the ideas around for a time; but now the cantina was filling up with soldiers, and we decided to move somewhere where we were less likely to be overheard. The streets were crowded, soldiers and girls, girls and soldiers, and the bars were doing fabulous business.

From a terrace above the town we could see the whole harbour. A cruiser and a destroyer were lying to their buoys, and beyond them, two U-boats. Even moored they looked deadly; I thought, they should have been our targets; and wondered only whether 'Fra Giuseppe' would find himself as welcome on board an Italian submarine as he had been on the *Giulio Cesare*.

Aldo brought me back to reality. Both he and Shep would be stevedoring aboard her next day. I would go on board myself later with a bundle of oil-soaked rags concealed under my robes. The three of us would meet on the shelter deck, and they would place the rags wrapped round bundles of wax-matches, against steam pipes in one of the holds before the hatches were battened down. We hadn't been able to find out when the ships were leaving, but according to rumour it should be within two or three days. This gave us time in hand if any snags cropped up.

The following day we went ahead with our plan. I met Aldo on board the *Cesare* and gave him the rags; then I toured the ship for a time, talking to the troops, as I had on the previous day. Already my presence was taken for granted; it would take more imagination than the average Italian naval officer possessed to connect the genial monk with a fire in Number One Hold. But that depended on how well Aldo and Shep had done their work.

As far as they could tell, they had set the scene: all we could do was wait and see. That evening we met as usual. Our conversation turned towards the future. I wanted to move on and try to get across to Sicily, but Aldo and Giovanni didn't think it would be easy to cross the Straits of Messina; and Shep had other ideas. He was thinking of settling down with Maria, who was a marvellous cook as well, he said. Anyway he didn't want to go to Sicily.

Obviously, I was deeply disappointed. We had come a long way together and had had many adventures; it seemed a pity to part now. But I wasn't too anxious about him; he had certainly learnt to take care of himself. As for me, I told myself, I'd started this thing on my own; I could finish it on my own.

But parting from Shep also meant parting from the others. They decided to go back to their homes. It's easy to talk about leaving friends, but when the time actually comes it can be terribly painful. I had made many during my journey, but of them all, Aldo, Giovanni, Shep and Gino – poor Gino – were the closest, if only because of our raid on the docks at Bari and the latest one, on the *Cesare*. We'd been together for some weeks now, and we'd become very close. Aldo said he hoped we should see the results of our latest 'job' before we left. We all had a lot to drink, and when at last I went to my room I must have fallen asleep right away, for I didn't hear Shep come in.

I was awoken abruptly next morning by Aldo suddenly bursting into the room in a great state of excitement. The docks were in an uproar; there was a fire on the *Cesare*. The watch had noticed that the decks were hot, and when he investigated, he smelled smoke. He raised the alarm and the hatches were opened. Immediately there was an explosion, and this had set off more fires. There had been so much confusion that the blaze was just about out of control. Most people had only been concerned with getting off the ship to safety, and this hadn't left enough on board to fight the fire. One thing we'd overlooked – the position of the magazine; and by the time it was in danger all the ammunition had been taken ashore. Otherwise we might really have blown her sky-high.

As it was, the damage was enough to hold up her sailing date indefinitely, so we were well satisfied. A mass of stores and equipment had been destroyed, but casualties were light. I had to go and see for myself; but when I tried to get through under the pretext of helping the wounded, I found the area cordoned off, and only military firemen allowed near the docks. I just got a glimpse of the ship; she seemed to be smouldering nicely.

Back in the cantina, people were talking of nothing else but the *Cesare*; the rumour had got about that the fire had been started by someone smoking in the holds. It wasn't too far from the truth. We ordered wine and celebrated our second success – the third for Shep and me. We drank to our collaboration, and to meeting in the future. Shep made me promise to keep in touch with him, and I said I would. I never saw him again.

Before I could move on, I had to kit myself up; above all

I needed boots. I'd had an idea, and the next morning I went to the quartermaster's store at the docks, which was outside the cordoned-off area, and asked if he could fit me up. It was a long shot, for boots were like gold-dust; but, overcome by my holy manner – and my disintegrating footwear – he took pity on me, and even added some socks and other things to go with them, and all gratis. When I went back to the cantina and showed my friends, they were convinced that my disguise as a monk was the greatest invention since the wheel. Every single thing I'd got was on ration, and most were virtually unobtainable.

I went up and packed, and we said our goodbyes.

Chapter Twenty

ALDO had told me to make for Taranto, which was only about 40 miles from Brindisi; from there he was sure I should get a ride most if not all of the way to Reggio, another 200 odd miles. And he was right. Very soon after leaving Brindisi, I was picked up by a truck going to Cosenza. It turned out to be a mixed blessing, for I quickly discovered that the driver, whose name was Stefano, was an ardent fascist, and I had to put up with an endless paean of praise for Mussolini and all his works.

I was quite glad to get away from him; but my next lift was, in some ways, even more trying. The driver had a woman with him, a brazen creature with dark hair, heavy make-up, and a powerful animal smell. She reminded me of the tarts I'd seen in Alex; even more so when, in the enforced intimacy of the cab, she started rubbing her leg against mine in a manner that left nothing to the imagination, and did nothing whatsoever for my vows. Finally, she gave me up as a hopeless case, and she and the driver went and had it off in the bushes, leaving me to my thoughts – which were not at all monastic.

However, that particular ride got me, more dead than alive, to Reggio di Calabria; and from there the ferries ran across the Straits to Sicily. I walked to the docks and in the failing light I could see the island across the water, and the lights of Messina. Illogically, I felt that my escape would be complete, once I had crossed that narrow strip of sea, and all the tensions of my year on the run were like a knot inside me. I wished I hadn't wasted so much time on the way . . . and yet, had it been wasted? The train, the oil dump, the *Cesare*, the friends I had made, the months of pretence? No, not entirely wasted.

There were a lot of people waiting to board the ferry, and I joined the end of the line. Guards were examining all papers, but this no longer worried me. It had happened too often before. Ahead of me, an elderly couple were struggling with a collection of large bundles. I offered to help, not purely out of kindness, I'm afraid. The couple were reluctant, but I insisted and finally the old lady gave me one of the more awkward ones. Just as I'd hoped, when my turn came to go through the gates, the guards and ticket-collector simply took one look at me, smiled, and waved me through. I saw the old dears settled – they were on their way to Palermo, they told me – and went out on deck. It was good to be aboard, on what felt like the last lap of my journey.

During one of the stops on the way from Brindisi, I had gone, as usual, to the church – one of the most beautiful I'd ever seen – and fallen into conversation with the priest. When he'd heard I was going to Sicily, he'd told me to be sure to look up a friend of his in Catania, Father Orso. I remembered this now; and whenever anyone asked me my destination, I gave Catania. I wasn't sure if I would ever reach it – I'd been sidetracked so often before – but I convinced myself that that was where I was going.

The ferry didn't take long to cross the Straits. As soon as I set foot on Sicilian soil, I felt strangely safe. It was 14 June, 1943; and it had taken me almost a year to get there.

*

I found that I could catch a bus to Catania from the centre of Messina. I made my way to the bus station, where there was one just about to leave. It was already almost full up.

The people were different from the Italians I had met on the mainland, smaller and darker, and I noticed that the men sat, while the women stood. Italian gallantry, it seemed, stopped short at the Straits. There was one empty window seat, and I made for it. The bus quickly filled to capacity, and we pulled out of the station.

I dozed off and woke to find we were arriving in Taormina. The driver announced that there would be a short stop, so I got out to stretch my legs. It was still warm, although it was late evening, and if I hadn't paid the bus fare I would willingly have walked the rest of the way to Catania.

Taormina is situated on cliffs overlooking the Straits of Messina as they merge with the Ionian Sea. The Italian mainland is only about 50 miles away, and I felt it was still too close for comfort. It was like a sudden spasm of superstition, the feeling that, after all, something might go wrong, that, even now, I might betray myself.

We were hustled back to the bus and I found I had lost my window seat; instead I wedged myself between two small Sicilians who looked like bandits, more Arabic than Italian. The driver set off as if he were escaping from a hold-up. As we rocketed along, lurching and rattling over the rough roads, I was offered some cheese and vino by one of the other passengers. I accepted it gratefully; I had to go easy with what little money I had left, because I wasn't sure when or if I could get any more. I could always scrounge a bed and a meal, but money was something else.

The heat and the wine made me drowsy and I dozed off again. I woke to find that we were approaching Catania. I was glad to get off the bus and away from the odour of garlic and sweaty bodies. I made for the nearest cafe to freshen up and find out how to get to the church of Father Orso. The people, I found, spoke a totally different dialect from that on the mainland; faster and more guttural than the Italian I was used to; just as the girls in the street were darker, and extremely beautiful. I greeted them as I passed and received flashing smiles in return.

I found the church without difficulty, and went inside. The decorations were magnificent; there were gold, silver and mosaic everywhere. It seemed strange when the people themselves were so poor. I was gazing round when a priest came up to me and introduced himself as Father Orso. I told him that I had been sent to him by Father Molinari; apparently they had been to seminary together, but hadn't seen each other for some time, and he was glad to have news of him.

He offered to put me up, and took me to a house next to the church belonging to a Signora Gallo. She showed me my room, but when I asked her how much it would cost, Father Orso interrupted, telling me not to worry, it would be taken care of. Nobody had asked me any questions about myself, which was strange; but I was so tired I didn't care. I went to bed and slept like a log.

*

I had arranged to see Father Orso the following morning. I woke late, for Signora Gallo, finding me so exhausted the previous night, had let me sleep on. After breakfast I took a walk in the town. There was plenty to see, for Catania is a very old city, with some beautiful buildings. I bought some postcards and sent one to Assunta, and one to Shep, in which I asked him to remember me to Aldo and the others. There was something that tickled me in the idea of an escaped PoW sending postcards like any tourist.

I had made it a rule to confide in the priests I met on my travels, and I obeyed it once more with Father Orso. Like the others, he did not seem particularly surprised, and he was, like them, largely sympathetic. I told him that I felt safe in Sicily and would like to stay there and await events. As it turned out, I didn't have to wait very long.

I stayed with Father Orso for a time, and through him I got to know a wealthy Sicilian family called Marchi. The father, Don Lorenzo, was an ardent fascist; his 18-year-old daughter, Magdalena, was a peach to look at, and a bitch in every other respect. Because of her father's wealth and position, no man was good enough for her; but being all too well aware of her desirability, she taunted every man who came to the house, even Father Orso and myself. There was a boy who worked for her father who was crazy about her. He was about 20, and his name was Enzo; he would do anything she asked and she treated him like dirt.

One evening Don Lorenzo invited Father Orso and me to dinner. His hospitality was fantastic; but it became obvious very soon that he used it to give him the chance of showing off his wealth, and expounding his views on fascism. He was convinced of the Axis's ultimate success in the war; their defeats in Russia and Africa he waved aside as being temporary setbacks. The deciding factor would be the battle for Europe; when that battle was joined, the superiority of the nazis and fascisti would tell. It was impossible to argue with him; but I had a shrewd idea that if the Allies ever occupied Sicily, his little world would crumble like a sand-castle. The citizens of Catania would take his property; and Enzo, I was sure, would take his daughter.

But for the time being, he felt secure in his opinion and his ostentation; and when, at last, Father Orso said it was time we were going, Don Lorenzo offered us the use of his limousine; but Father Orso said we would rather walk. I saw the car outside the villa. It was a Bugatti: I would love to have brought it back to England.

After we got back to the house, I stayed for a long time at the window of my room looking out. It was a beautiful clear night, and I amused myself by identifying the stars that burned so brightly in the Mediterranean sky. All was calm, still and peaceful. Then, from far to the southward, there came a series of vivid flashes followed by a heavy rumbling sound. A thunderstorm, I thought, and stood waiting for the rain to begin. But though the thunder continued, no rain fell, and this puzzled me. Was it an air raid, possibly on Syracuse? The streets below started to fill with people, all very excited. Could it be Etna erupting? But Etna was to the north-west, and this came from the south. At that moment Signora Gallo burst into my room. She was hysterical.

'Fra Giuseppe, it's the end of the world! We are all to be punished for our sins!'

I calmed her down as best I could, and went out. The church was full of people praying and wailing; it seemed that they really did think it was the end of the world. The less superstitious were ready to accept that it was a raid; but as Father Orso and I pointed out, in that case we should hear the aircraft and the German ack-ack batteries, and there was neither.

It wasn't until an hour or two later that we learned the truth. That night was the 5–6 July, 1943, and at 3 a.m. the Mayor of Catania, Don Antonio Bello, complete with his chain of office, came to the church and announced that the Americans and British had launched an invasion on Sicily, and had landed at Syracuse and Gela.

I was stunned with joy. This was the best news I had heard since my escape. The Catanians, on the other hand, were of a different opinion. Panic seized them, and there was a rush to get away from the town and into the mountains, where they thought they would be safe. Police and soldiers were trying to restore order outside, but it was useless; and the mood of imminent catastrophe wasn't soothed by army trucks racing through the streets, heading out of Catania.

Syracuse was only about 30 miles south of Catania, and it looked as if I should soon be within a few miles of my own people. This was what I had been waiting for, and now it was here, I didn't know what to do. Even in their panic, most of the people seemed more happy than upset at the invasion; there were shouts of welcome for the Allies and I couldn't figure out if the Sicilians were two-faced, or were genuinely glad to know that the British and Americans had landed. I had the feeling I could have openly said I was English and been treated as a hero; but caution prevailed. There were too many Germans about.

In the City Hall, the Mayor and other town officials were discussing whether to evacuate Catania or sit tight until the Allied armies arrived. There were a lot of German soldiers around; they were setting up machine-gun posts and covering the main crossroads with tanks, which suggested that they were preparing to defend the town. There were a few nasty incidents. A German soldier had been found in an alley with his throat cut, which was hardly likely to improve Italo-German relations, which were never good; and a girl had been badly beaten up, probably for fraternizing with the Germans in the past.

Father Orso, I discovered, was already in touch with an anti-fascist group which, it seemed, had been waiting for such a moment as this. They had all gathered at his house, about twenty of them. Some were very young, no more than 16 or 17, but they all had one thing in common, they would do anything in their power to impede the Germans defending Catania. They had been promised the moon by Mussolini, but when they had been made to turn in their gold wedding rings and other jewellery to support him, they had become bitterly opposed to his régime.

I suggested that we concentrate on blocking the railways and roads leading in and out of Catania. In fact, the roads were already choked with refugees coming in from the south on anything with wheels – farm carts, bicycles, prams, dilapidated trucks and cars, anything that could be pulled, pushed or ridden. We spread the word among them to stay put, as the advancing Allied armies would not harm them. Some tried to double back, only to meet head-on others coming up behind them. This really caused confusion, and soon satisfactorily blocked the main road into Catania from the south.

There had been no rehearsal for the other things Father Orso's little band did, but they went about their work with a cold efficiency that would have done credit to trained commandos. They cut telephone and power lines, and chopped down telegraph poles; and I've no doubt cut quite a few more German throats in between times. As a kid I had heard stories about the Mafia, and I had only half believed them; now I wasn't so sure.

One of them had a Lüger pistol he had taken from a German soldier; I didn't ask him if he had killed to get the gun, but I couldn't imagine a live German giving his Lüger away. The others all wanted arms, of course, and someone suggested a raid on the barracks of the *carabiniere*. This was agreed upon, and ten of them left to carry it out. An hour or two later they came back loaded with rifles, revolvers and plenty of ammunition. The armoury was on the ground floor, and they had simply filed through the bars on the window and helped themselves. There was so much confusion everywhere that no one had interfered with them, and they'd got clean away with their hoard.

I could see that the invading forces were going to find useful allies, and the Germans some implacable enemies, among the local population. My own aim was to get myself nearer the front. Father Orso strongly advised me to stay in Catania and wait to be liberated; but I had another, and I thought better, idea.

Chapter Twenty-one

My scheme was to go direct to the German HQ, which occupied the theatre, and try and persuade them to help me repatriate myself. Father Orso volunteered to come with me. We had to go through the centre of the town to get there; cars had been turned over and set alight, and a bus was lying on its side, blocking the main street. None of the officials seemed to know what to do. The Germans were trying to enlist their help, and the civilians were doing the same. The police, being Sicilian born, were divided between their duty as policemen and loyalty to their country. I didn't envy them their dilemma.

At the German HQ we were stopped by two sentries. I asked to see the Commandant, but this was refused. A lieutenant came over and asked what was wrong. I told him I wanted to leave Catania and go south to where the invasion had taken place, to see if I could be of any help with the German wounded. He relented a little at that and said he would give me a pass to get me out of Catania.

'What about transport?'

But at that he jibbed; he couldn't do anything for me. He told me that there had been landings near Avola, close to Syracuse, but that I couldn't go directly there because it was too dangerous. I could, however, go to a place called Noto, which was still behind the front line. I said that I would go anywhere where I could help – without mentioning whom

I wanted to help. He gave me a pass, signed and stamped it, and we left to rejoin the partisans at the priest's house.

The band had grown by this time, and numbered almost a hundred. One had to admire them. They were perfectly willing to give their lives, if necessary, to hamper the Axis and thereby assist the Allies' post-invasion advance.

They had plenty of opportunities. Catania itself was rapidly being turned into a German stronghold. More tanks had been brought in, and nearly every building had a machine-gun post in it. There were also anti-tank guns dotted around the streets. The rebels already had plans for them, so I left them to it. We went over the main points in the city where we could do most damage: the railway, the docks, power lines, the auxiliary generators belonging to the Germans, and, of course, the German HQ.

The cell was divided into two, fifty being employed for important jobs of this kind, and the rest roaming round and causing as much confusion as they could, without doing any substantial damage, but acting as a decoy for the big jobs. They had a number of spontaneous successes.

One of our group, Egisto, pulled a stunt of this kind entirely on his own. He was driving a truck loaded with about ten tons of hardcore just outside the town when a German staff car overtook him. The road was narrow and winding. He let the car go by, and then, racing after it, sounded his horn repeatedly to make them think something was wrong. The staff car pulled over to let him pass, he rammed it, and somehow managed to tip his truck over on top of it. Egisto escaped with scratches, but four German officers and the NCO driver were killed.

It has been said that the Italians were not good fighters; but when they felt the cause was right, there were none better. The individuals I'd come across had all responded quickly enough when the opportunity was offered them; and of them all, there had only been one I'd doubts about. His name was

Sergio; and Therese, Egisto's wife, warned me not to trust him. I wasn't sure why. He hadn't been present at any of our secret meetings, but I hoped he didn't know the truth about me, because I'd heard that the Gestapo had been asking him questions about certain people, and had told him to listen to gossip and report back to them, particularly details of any partisan activities.

It was through him that I received a polite message to go, at my convenience, to the German Commandant's office. Forewarned, in this case, was forearmed, and I decided to be extremely wary when I presented myself at the SS HQ, to be received very courteously by an NCO receptionist. The Commandant was a major, resplendent in black SS uniform and highly polished jackboots. He offered me a seat and a drink, both of which I accepted, and, coming straight to the point, asked me in Italian where I had come from and what I was doing in Catania. I replied that I'd been travelling around Italy for some time, and that going among the people was obligatory for members of my Order. If it hadn't been for the invasion, I said, I would probably have been on my way back north by now, to a monastery where I could continue my studies.

He nodded, and sat looking at me in silence for several minutes. This made me nervous, as he no doubt intended it should; I hadn't come up against his kind before. At last he reached over to the intercom and said something in German to the NCO in the outer office. Father Orso's name was mentioned. What the hell was he up to? He still didn't say anything to me. He got up and went to the window. He looked out for a while, then came over and offered me a cigarette.

'I don't smoke,' I said. And then, 'Am I free to go?'

He looked at me again. 'No. Wait.'

I sat and sipped my wine, and tried to look as unconcerned as my pounding heart would let me. If he hadn't believed my story, could I get his gun from him? I was ready to kill him if necessary, though I doubted if I'd get out of the building alive if I did. Anyway, I couldn't be sure what game he was playing with me. I waited.

The intercom buzzed, and Father Orso was shown in. The major greeted him formally, then:

'How well do you know Fra Giuseppe, Father?'

The priest said that I'd been sent to him by an old friend, and that he would vouch for me completely. He calmly ádded several circumstantial details of my travels and my work with wounded servicemen. It sounded very convincing, and after a pause the Commandant nodded.

'Very well. It wouldn't be the first time the cloth has been used to conceal a fifth columnist. You may go.'

We bowed and left, just two priests who had incurred the passing suspicions of the SS; but I could feel the Commandant's hostile glare boring into the back of my neck, and I didn't breathe freely until we were out of the building and half a mile up the street. Suddenly, and for the first time since Shep was taken off for questioning after the train incident, I felt perilously vulnerable. And so nearly home. I had always dreaded the thought of falling foul of the Germans; and now that I'd had a mild taste of their power, I knew why.

As we walked soberly back to the priest's house, I hugged my luck and touched the crucifix that, for a year, I had worn round my neck like a talisman. I had my pass: it was time I made the final effort to reach the invading armies. After all, they had come half-way to meet me!

When I announced that I was leaving, Egisto and the others immediately bent their minds to the problems. Transport was the first; a monk couldn't be seen driving a truck or even a cart – a pity, because vehicles were plentiful. Then somebody suggested that I get myself a mule. At first I didn't take this idea seriously; but the others liked it. As a mode of travel it was reliable, and in character; and a mule would take the weight off my feet, even if other parts of my anatomy suffered instead. And so it was agreed, and someone went off to beg, buy, borrow or steal a suitable beast.

Early the next morning found me on my way south to Syracuse astride an animal so bony and dejected it hardly seemed fair to ride it. It progressed with a curious swaying motion which constantly threatened my balance and didn't help my head one bit. We had had a farewell party the night before, and my glass had been filled and refilled many times. The road was swarming with refugees struggling up from the south, away from the continuous gunfire. They travelled in carts and on foot, carrying bundles or pushing their possessions in prams and handcarts, thousands of them, straggling all over the road. These people only knew one thing, they wanted to get away from the rumble of the guns which had been going on, virtually non-stop, for almost a week. German motorcycle combinations with machine-guns mounted on the sidecars were patrolling the column, trying to keep it moving and in some kind of order; as well try and control a herd of cattle. Every now and then a soldier would jump down and drive some helpless refugee out of the road in front of them. I and my mule were fighting against this human tide, and after a short time I left the road and made my way through the fields alongside.

I came to a farm near Lentini, where I stopped and asked for some water. The farmer gave me wine instead, which helped neither my hangover nor my thirst, and also some bread and meat, which I badly needed. When I told him I was heading south for the battle zone he became quite agitated; but when I asked him why he had not joined the exodus, he said that the farm was all he had, it was the only home he had ever known, and he could not bring himself to leave. I prayed that he would still have a home when the battle had passed, and that his farmhouse wouldn't be a pile of rubble, the site of a machine-gun nest, and a mortuary for the bodies of the troops who would die defending it. But there was no point in trying to persuade him to leave. The peasant farmer who loses his land loses everything. Better to sit tight and take a chance. I gave the mule some hay and water and continued on my way.

Later on that day I came to a village called Priolo. I could hear the big guns very plainly now. The village had been largely evacuated, and the few stores were boarded up in a pathetic effort to save them from being looted. At the Prefecture, which was still manned, they sent me to the cantina, which, surprisingly, was also open, and I was given a room and a meal. The mule was put in the stables at the back, and watered and fed. The cantina was almost full, and I asked the owner why these people hadn't joined the refugees. He said that they were all convinced the Allies would not harm them when they came. I was glad he felt so confident that the Allies were coming, and asked him why. He said that the invasion had been a complete success; beach-heads had been established all along the coast from Syracuse to Pachino, and the Americans had landed on the south side of the island and were fighting for Agrigento. The pictures of Mussolini which hung on the walls of the cantina had been broken, and fascist posters in the village had been defaced with red paint and anti-fascist slogans. As in Catania, the people of Priolo seemed ripe for a revolution; and it occurred to me that this information might be useful to the Allies – whenever I succeeded in reaching them.

From Priolo I plodded on, circumventing Syracuse, to the town of Noto. Invasion or not, the road signs were still intact, and there was no difficulty about finding the way. It took me the best part of the day to reach Noto, and that night I slept at the house of one Giorgio Bocchino, who gladly gave me a room, fed both me and the mule, and promised to wake me early next morning.

He did – at dawn! I'd wanted an early start, and I got it. This was probably going to be my last day on the road, and I was deeply excited at the prospect of being once more with my own people. Perhaps I should be hailed as a bit of a hero; I felt I certainly had a fund of information, about both Italy and Sicily, that would be welcome.

The refugees on the road now were not civilians, but the remnant of a fleeing army. A sergeant I spoke to said that the 'enemy' were fully established on the coast, and 'we' were falling back to make a stand at Catania, where the Germans were sending reinforcements. The casualties had been heavy, and the front was being held by Italian troops who had never been in action before. The amount of wrecked equipment, tanks, armoured troop carriers, field guns and the growing number of dead men and animals, bore him out. The stench, in that blazing Mediterranean sun, was nauseating, for the dead were lying where they had fallen. The whole area was pitted with craters, probably the result of the original soften-ing-up bombardment on the first morning of the invasion. That was over a week ago. Most of the corpses had been stripped of their clothing and weapons, and the children were wearing army boots. Sporadic firing was still going on, closer now, and I knew I must be getting near the front line.

My mule suddenly came to a dead stop, and, despite kick-ing, punching and shouting, refused to budge. I looked around for a stick, and then saw the reason. Ahead of us a dead mule was being torn apart by dogs. Its stomach had been dragged out, and they were devouring its entrails. It was a sight so savage and horrible that I was violently sick on the spot. Close by, another mule was so bloated that I half-expected it to burst. My poor old fellow willingly al-lowed himself to be turned and led away from the scene, but one couldn't escape the stench; it was everywhere. And to think that, once, I had balked at latrine duty at Campo 303!

In spite of the detour round these horrors I made good

time. The shelling had stopped; now that I was so close to the occupied area, I was struck by the lack of activity. I had expected to run into troops, to be shot at, or at least challenged; instead there was this odd limbo of silence and death. Expectant, and a little afraid, I plodded on.

A farmer burying some cattle which had been killed in the bombardment told me that the British were close by, and that a mopping-up patrol had passed him not long before. He pointed after them and I followed his directions. A strange dreamlike feeling of unreality smothered me. If I'd imagined anything, it was lying in a ditch with a battle raging round me, trying desperately to choose the right moment to make myself known. Instead, I was all alone in this stinking wilderness of corpses, and the battle had passed me by.

Chapter Twenty-two

I CAME to a village. There were tanks in what was left of the square, and a group of soldiers next to one of them. I made my way towards them, and saw that they were men of the Highland Division. None of them took any notice as I approached. Then a sergeant stepped forward and asked quite civilly, 'What can I do for ye, Padre?'

'Will you take me to your CO?' I said.

'Aye. Mebbe. What d'ye want of him, may I ask?'

'I'm an escaped British prisoner-of-war,' I said.

'Och aye.'

If I'd claimed to be a Martian, it wouldn't have carried any less credibility as far as he was concerned, and I noticed he kept his gun in his hand.

'Come along.'

Outside the police station, which was doing duty as Company HQ, he stopped.

'Wait here, please.'

A minute or two later, he put his head round the door. 'This way.'

Inside were two British officers, a major and a lieutenant, the village policeman, the sergeant who had brought me there, and a corporal. They gave me a seat and the major said:

'Sergeant tells me you're an escaped prisoner-of-war.'

'That's correct, sir,' I replied.

He grunted. 'Can I have your service details?'

I gave him my name, rank and number and told him I was T124X, ex-*Agamemnon*. He wrote it all down.

'And which prison camp were you at?'

'Campo 303, Pavia.'

'Any of your shipmates there with you?'

'Yes,' and I gave him the names of Ken, Ace and Nugget.

'I see. And when did you escape?'

'August last year.'

'Yes. And *how* did you escape?'

I gave him a brief outline of my adventures.

'Remarkable.' He finished his notes, then picked up the telephone. 'HQ?' He gave them the gist of the matter. 'I'll send him along to you then, shall I? Right. Will do.' He put the phone down and turned to me.

'By the way, have you any means of identification?'

'No. I left everything in the camp.'

'Yes, quite. Pity.'

'Why a pity?'

'Well, frankly, they may not believe you. Look at it from their point of view. A man dressed as a monk strolls into our lines claiming to be a PoW. No identification, nothing. In the middle of a battle. Could be an enemy agent, anything. I'm inclined to think you're genuine, but I'm not a bit sure they will. They'll want proof.'

I felt very flattened. Then I told him about the stand the Germans were planning to make at Catania, and the indications of popular support for the Allies which I had seen there and elsewhere.

'Divisional HQ will be interested in that,' he said; and then, 'By the way, do you speak Italian?'

I smiled. '*Poco*,' I said, and started a rapid conversation with the policeman.

'Splendid. We badly need interpreters to cope with the Eyetye prisoners.'

137

The vision of freedom, which had rather receded during our conversation, started to return. Major Geoffrey Moorhouse, at least, seemed to be on my side.

*

Next morning I was told to find my way to Divisional HQ under my own steam. This struck me as very funny; I was supposed to be a German agent, but was expected to find HQ for myself, using my own transport! I felt they might at least have laid on a jeep and escort and done the job properly. As it was, I'd have to get the old mule going again.

'I think it's disgusting,' said Corporal McCleod, who had woken me. 'If I'd been in your place,' he said, 'I'd have stayed where I was, with the signorinas. Can ye no go back where you came from?'

'It's too late now,' I said.

I was given directions, and I and the mule pushed off. I was really mad; depression and disappointment had given way to sheer fury. I knew one thing. I wasn't going to take any bull from anybody. If they thought I was an enemy agent, fine, let them prove it. They'd have to check up on me first, and in the meantime they could feed me. I was sure I'd have received different treatment from the enemy if I had been on their side. I was so angry I couldn't see how funny it was: for the first time in a year I was among Englishmen, a moment I'd looked forward to for so long, and here I was, being treated either as a dangerous spy or a harmless lunatic. At least the exasperation kept me going until I reached HQ, which was a large tented area in an olive wood.

The men stared at me, and I must have looked a hell of a sight – a ragged monk riding an even raggeder mule. At the HQ tent I was kept waiting, and had a further chance to stoke up my indignation. I was hungry and dirty, and I felt as if the whole world was against me. Finally a captain appeared and led me inside. The tent was full of top brass –

colonels and lieutenant-colonels, and a full general, Graham Walker, 51st Highland Division.

We went through the rigmarole again; and at the end of it the general said my identification would have to be verified. In the meantime I would just have to sit tight.

'All I want at the moment,' I said, 'is to get cleaned up and have something to eat.'

'See to it, Captain Thomas.'

The captain took me outside and handed me over to a sergeant, who handed me over to a corporal, who showed me the ablutions tent, where I washed, and the mess tent, where I was given a meal. What muck! After what I had been eating for the past year, it was garbage, and I said so.

Having found my own way there, I was now put under guard, a prisoner with the prospect of remaining so until my identity was established. When I mentioned that I had come right through their lines without once being challenged, and I didn't think much of their security, it caused quite a rumpus but did me no good. I remained a prisoner. As for the blokes and the NCOs, their attitude was 'Serve you right, you should have stayed with the signorinas!'

*

This went on for three days, during which I continued to wear my disintegrating habit and remained under surveillance inside the camp. The story of my adventures soon got about, and I didn't lack an audience, either for them or for my resentment. But my inside information on Catania was, as far as I could gather, completely ignored.

On the fourth day I was taken to the HQ tent. General Walker was there with an Aide. He dismissed the guard.

'Well, Orna, you'll be glad to hear that I've received a message from the Admiralty verifying your identity, and the fact that you were reported a prisoner-of-war.'

139

'Thank you very much, sir,' I said, being unable to think of anything else.

'You will report to HMS *Bulolo*, HQ ship, Combined Operations, in Syracuse, forthwith.'

'Yes, sir.'

He gave me a curious, masked look which I couldn't interpret, and then a twinkle came briefly to his eyes.

'No doubt they will issue you with an – er – other uniform. That's all. Good luck.'

And that was that.

*

HMS *Bulolo*, I soon discovered, was a new kind of naval animal, a floating radar station and headquarters ship; and as such, she was stiff with brasshats of all three services. Just my luck, I thought, as, still in my robes, I was put aboard one of her boats in Syracuse harbour under the stares of the waterfront loungers and the unbelieving look of the coxswain.

'At ease, chum,' I said to him out of the side of my mouth as I settled myself in the sternsheets and arranged my robe decorously round me. 'I'm as English as you are.'

His jaw dropped another three-eighths of an inch; he obviously wasn't accustomed to being addressed in Cockney by Italian monks. The officer in charge of the boat was polite but distant, and I felt like telling him I held the newly-created rank of Leading Friar.

Once on board, I was wheeled along to the upper deck by the Regulating Petty Officer.

'Where're we going?' I asked, as we entered the more rarefied atmosphere of the senior officers' quarters. 'Captain's defaulters?'

'Admiral wants to see you,' he replied; and added under his breath, 'Gawd knows why.'

I could have told him; but after my reception by the army, and their total disinterest in my story (except for the *signorinas*), I decided not to. He probably wouldn't have believed me, anyway.

In the Admiral's suite, we were met by a flag lieutenant, resplendent in his gold epaulettes; and after a few moments, he led me next door.

'This is Leading Steward Orna, sir, ex-*Agamemnon*, sunk off Tobruk last summer. Found his way into our lines four days ago.'

From the moment of that first meeting with Rear Admiral Tom Troubridge, I began to feel differently about my return. There was something in his broad, humorous face, and in his deep voice which so often had a chuckle lurking in it, that immediately restored in me a sense of my own reality.

'Ah yes. Sit down, sit down. Cup of tea?'

When I was settled, he went on: 'Well, Orna, we know all about you. We're desperately short of people who can speak Italian. You can be useful to us as an interpreter. Now – ' he turned to Flags, 'call the yeoman, will you.' Then to me: 'I believe you have some information about the enemy's dispositions round Catania. Am I right?'

'Yes, sir,' I said. 'I spent several days in Catania, and I was in touch with anti-Fascist groups there.'

'Sounds interesting. Let's hear about it.'

With the yeoman of signals taking it all down in shorthand, and the Admiral nodding, occasionally putting in a question. I told him about the pro-Allied feeling I had encountered in Sicily, and as much as I could about the German build-up in Catania itself. 'I'm sure they mean to hold it,' I said.

'It certainly sounds like it,' the Admiral said. He dismissed the yeoman, and asked me a number of questions about my escape. Then he said: 'I shall see that your information reaches those to whom it can be of most use. Now, the Captain's secretary tells me you've been rated up to petty officer, so you'd better pay a visit to the slop chest and get yourself kitted up accordingly. For as long as we're here,

141

you'll hold yourself available to act as interpreter, either for me or for Major Klein of the American army ashore.'

I stood up and thanked him. He smiled. 'I've got a meeting with the Mayor at 0930 tomorrow morning. He doesn't speak a word of English, so I shall need your help.'

I left the cabin feeling, for the first time, that I was glad to have made it back.

*

Tropical kit felt strange after a year in a monk's robes – especially the shorts! – but one soon got used to it. I shaved off my beard, and got a rocket for doing so without the Captain's permission – though I hadn't asked anyone's permission to grow it in the first place! – and the following morning, and for the next few weeks while the ship remained in Syracuse, I dodged between the Admiral and the American city major's office ashore, as my services were required. Technically, I was still a petty officer steward; but interpreting had priority; and one day the Captain's secretary sent for me and told me my name had been put forward for promotion to sub lieutenant, and if it was approved, I should be shore-based as resident interpreter. This would have suited my book well, for as Major Klein spoke no Italian, and he was responsible for issuing permits to the local traders who applied to re-open their shops, I would have had a nice little operation going. It was encouraging how much it was worth to some of them. Unfortunately the ship sailed before the appointment came through, and I had to sail with her.

*

But for those few weeks I had a high old time. The oddity of my position, half steward, half confidant of high-ranking officers, was neatly illustrated one day when Admiral Troubridge took me ashore with him on some interpreting job or other. The flag lieutenant was with us, and a major or two, and we were walking across the main square of Syracuse on our way to the *sindaco*'s office when there was a yell from the policeman on point-duty.

'*Giuseppe! Come stai?*'

'*Domenico! Molto bene!*' I replied. '*E tu stesso?*'

'*Bene, bene!*'

The traffic came to an agonized halt during this exchange. As it sorted itself out, the Admiral turned to me, his eyebrows raised.

'What's all that about? And who's this "Giuseppe"?'

'That's me, sir. Italian for Joseph.'

'I see. Policeman's a pal of yours, is he?'

'That's right, sir.'

Then came the famous chuckle. 'You must have made many friends on your travels, Orna,' he observed drily.

'I did, sir; a great many, in all walks of life.'

And we proceeded on our way across the *piazza* in the dignified manner befitting the senior officers of the occupying power, and, of course, their temporary interpreter.